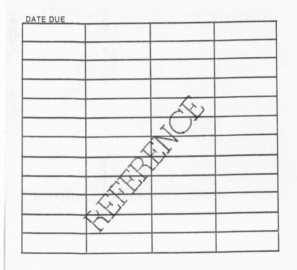

SUMMER OF TRIUMPH

Also by Hal Higdon

The Union Vs. Dr. Mudd

The Business Healers

The Crime of the Century: The Leopold and Loeb Case

Finding the Groove

Find the Key Man

Pro Football USA

On the Run From Dogs and People

Fitness After Forty

SUMMER OF TRIUMPH

HAL HIGDON

G. P. PUTNAM'S SONS, NEW YORK

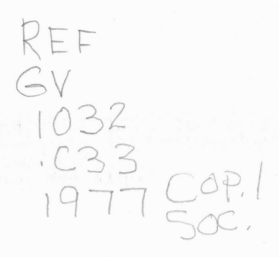
Copyright © 1977 by Hal Higdon

SBN: 399-11911-6

Library of Congress Cataloging in Publication Data

Higdon, Hal.
    Summer of triumph.

     1.   Caruthers, Jimmy. 2.   Automobile racing drivers--United States--Biography. I. Title.
GV1032.C33H53   1977   796.7'2'0924   [B]   77-2217

This book is dedicated to my mother-in-law,
Angela Tocci Musacchio,
a wonderful woman who treated me well.

Life is never gentle on the midget circuit. Maintaining the small, noisy cars is messy, tedious work. Drivers (and their mechanics) spend long hours traveling from city to city. Little money can be won. Only a few drivers—the ones who consistently finish in front—earn enough to justify the time and effort. The United States Auto Club Midget Car champion in any given year wins around $15,000 in prizes. Sponsors are difficult to find and keep. There is no pension plan in USAC as in professional baseball or football. There are no paid vacations.

Drivers run midgets because they love racing. They love the excitement, the thrill of competition. They love the sweet smell of fuel that lingers over the pits. They love the sounds, the harsh roar of unmuffled engines vibrating against their eardrums. They love the feel of the small cars, their twitchiness, the sensation of speed they experience. They love running in tight packs of five and six machines, swapping positions, banging wheels, sliding up and down the track in the corners. They love being brave. They even love the threat of injury, almost as though by challenging death they become more alive. They love things mechanical, the challenge of making pieces of machinery fit together and function efficiently. They love the adulation of the crowd, the programs thrust at them for autographs. They love the gum-chewing girls clad in tight jeans who hang around the pits hoping for a smile or a wave or something more. Particularly they love the girls.

"Hey, Jimmy. Sign my program."

"Sure I will. What's your name?"

"Mary Ann."

Best wishes to Mary Ann from Jimmy Caruthers.

Douglas James Caruthers, Jr., of Anaheim, California—although nobody knew him by his full name. He was Jimmy. "Jimmy Caruthers" was written in hand-lettered script on the helmet he wore in midget auto races from coast to coast. Jimmy was born on January 18, 1945, and was in his mid twenties, the summer of his life, when he came to the Midwest with his racer on a trailer. He was like lot of young drivers—and old drivers—who raced USAC circuit each summer. He wanted to win Indy.

"Hey, McClung!" he sometimes shouted at his friend, Jerry McClung.

"What is it now, Caruthers?"

"I'm going to win the big one."

"Yeah?"

"I'm going to win Indy. Sooner or later I'm going to do it."

"Goddamn, Caruthers, I think you will."

Nearly all those who join the midget circuit do so thinking someday they will step from the feisty machines with their miniature engines to the better powered championship cars driven at the Indianapolis Motor Speedway, the

pinnacle of the auto racing sport. For most, this is just illusion—a dream to dwell upon while traveling the long road
each summer. Some on the midget circuit are old, their illusions long faded. But Jimmy Caruthers still had his
dream—one he shared with many others.

Like many, he was a local champion from Southern California before he joined the United States Auto Club's
touring elite. The midget circuit is a circuit of local cham-
pions—the best drivers from places like Huron, Harrisburg, and Gardena who want to get away from places like
Huron, Harrisburg, and Gardena. They join USAC and
travel the country, racing three and four times a week,
hoping some rich car owner will recognize their talent and
send them to Indy next May. They suffer the fatigues and
hardships and perils of the hot, dusty summer, hoping
someday to find the right ride.

For all its hardships—perhaps because of those hardships—there is a certain attraction to the midget circuit.
The men and women—drivers, mechanics, wives, girl
friends—who travel the midget circuit possess a shared experience. They see each other every other night in a different location. They carry their neighborhood with them.
They become a traveling circus, a pack of Gypsies who pile
their gear into the pickup at the end of a night's racing on
Friday and reappear two hundred miles down the road
Saturday afternoon at another track, somehow looking eager and ready to race. Smiles on their faces and ready to
race. No money in their coveralls, but ready to race. The
scenery has changed; the faces remain the same.

Over the years they learn to cope with their environ-
ment. They come to the track carrying their comforts with
them—campers in which they can sleep and cook and sit
on while watching the race. Coolers stuffed with fried
chicken and cold beer. Drivers pool transportation, motel
rooms, and often female companionship. They also share

tools and parts and tips on how to drive different tracks—angles to take going into the corner, spring settings, tire compounds and threads.

Friendships made on the midget circuit become long-lasting friendships among people who have survived. It is a form of friendship almost unique in professional sports. Baseball and football players know their teammates but see their opponents only as shadows in the dugout across the field, shapes to be battled and conquered. Race drivers travel and live and party with those they battle. Among the regular battlers on the midget circuit, Jimmy Caruthers was one of the best liked.

Perhaps it was his disposition. He seemed to radiate good will. Jimmy Caruthers had twinkling eyes and a broad smile he flashed frequently. His blond hair was long, curly, dirty from working on automotive engines. He was short, stocky, muscular, yet with a bit of a belly because he enjoyed drinking beer.

Like many of the young breed of racers who toured the midget circuit in the late sixties and early seventies, Jimmy Caruthers came from a racing family. His father was Douglas James Caruthers, Sr., better known as Doug, sometimes also known as "Slug," or "Slugger," because of his easily ignitable temper and penchant for hurling things. It was said that Doug could place a wrench in a toolbox from a distance of ten paces—and he often did it.

Doug grew up in Texas and then moved to Kansas, where he ran whiskey during the Depression. In the forties he headed to California and opened a chain of gas stations, later started a mobile home business, and made a lot of money. He owned some property in Anaheim that Disneyland leased for a parking lot. He drove midgets in his spare time until, fearful for the security of his children, Doug let others drive his cars.

Doug's brother, Leonard, Jimmy's Uncle Red, also

owned midget cars, and Jimmy spent his childhood at racetracks, sneaking into the pits to be close to the cars and drivers. When he was eight, his father built him a quarter midget, which he drove on a tenth-of-a-mile track behind the family mobile home lot in Anaheim. Jimmy Bryan, Doug's driver, supervised Jimmy Caruthers' training, teaching him how to power-slide through the turns. He drove quarter midgets against other youngsters like Mike Mosley, Swede Savage, Johnny Parsons, Jr., and Pancho Carter. At age eleven he won a national quarter midget race in Phoenix, Arizona. His brother, Danny, four years younger, also drove the tiny cars.

It was a relatively safe sport, the only person injured being Jimmy Bryan. The older driver could not fit in the cockpit of a quarter midget, but one day, as a lark, hopped on the tail of one of the cars and tried racing it around the track. Bryan fell off and broke his arm. In addition to his great driving skill, Jimmy Bryan possessed a wild streak. Jimmy Caruthers, as he grew older, seemed to inherit both the driving skill and the wild streak from the man he admired.

Jimmy's father frequently spent summers racing in the Midwest. Jimmy Bryan drove for him; so did other famous drivers. Doug rented a home near the Indianapolis Motor Speedway and garaged his race car in Gasoline Alley at the track. Jimmy traveled with his father, encountering the sons of others in racing, including Billy Vukovich and Gary Bettenhausen.

Billy's father, Bill Vukovich, won the Indy 500 in 1953 and 1954. He was leading the race in 1955 when he crashed and died. Jimmy Bryan won the Indy 500 in 1958; two years later he died in a wreck in Langhorne, Pennsylvania. Gary's father, Tony Bettenhausen, never won the 500, but did finish second. He died while testing another driver's car in practice for the 500 in 1960.

Jimmy's mother, La Vey Caruthers, lost her enthusiasm

for auto racing because of such incidents and soon refused to attend races anymore. "I've seen too many of our friends get killed," she told Doug. She would not watch auto racing on television for fear of something happening to someone they knew, even when the televised event occurred weeks earlier. Jimmy's father and mother drifted apart, separated, and eventually divorced. The family thus became another one of racing's victims, although both Doug and La Vey (Johnny, as her friends called her) remained close to their four children.

Jimmy did not worry about the dangers of auto racing—or if he did, he kept his fears welled deep within him. He knew he wanted to be a race driver.

At one point his mother financed flying lessons for her son, hoping an interest in airplanes would keep him away from racing. Doug considered flying *more* dangerous than racing. Jimmy learned to fly, obtained an FAA license to fiy not only fixed-wing planes, but also helicopters—but this still did not subdue his interest in racing cars.

As a teenager Jimmy served his apprenticeship in stock cars and three-quarter midgets. Though under age, he disguised his birth date so he could race. He competed in his first USAC midget event on March 25, 1967, when Bobby Unser could not come in from Albuquerque to drive Doug's car. Jimmy, twenty-two years old, won the feature event, beating Mel Kenyon and Billy Vukovich. When he returned home that night, his mother handed him an envelope from the Department of the Army. He was drafted.

He continued to race in the service at the officer's club at Fort Wachutka. Not all hazards are on racetracks. One day, while cleaning the swimming pool with a long pole, he brushed it against an overhead power line. A bolt of electricity shot through him. The shock knocked Jimmy unconscious. Had not someone quickly revived him, he might have died.

Jimmy almost won the Arizona sprint car championship,

but the Army shipped him to Taiwan before the last race of the season, and he finished third in points. He returned from the service and got married to a girl named Sally, who was blonde and beautiful. But the lure of auto racing remained upon him. Doug had a new midget car for Jimmy to drive. It was painted yellow and it, too, was beautiful. So Jimmy went off racing that summer in the Midwest. He loved his new wife, but he loved racing even more. His marriage with Sally seemed threatened almost from the beginning. Because of the constant traveling, very few race drivers succeed as drivers and husbands simultaneously.

Jimmy failed to win any races during the summer of 1969 and flipped his car several times. When he arrived home in the fall, after the end of the Midwest season, he began to consider abandoning his racing career. Don Edmunds, a car builder on the West Coast, teased him: "You better go into the trailer business like your old man, get rich, then become a racer."

"Yeah," thought Jimmy. "Maybe I'll settle down."

Doug, however, warned his son against quitting prematurely. "As much as I'd like to see you go get a job and forget it, I know damn well you won't, so you might as well give it another shot."

Jimmy also sought advice from his Uncle Red, who used to sneak him cigarettes when he was younger. Uncle Red, also in the mobile home business, told Jimmy he could work for him any time, but he should not do it if he had any doubts concerning his racing career. "Find out what you want to do." advised Uncle Red, "Then do it."

Jimmy gave the matter some thought—but not too much. He knew what he wanted to do, and that was to race, drive a championship car at Indy, and eventually win that race. That was his single goal, and anything else that got in the way would have to be shoved aside. Jimmy realized it was selfish of him, but he was under the control of forces that even he did not understand.

The decision to continue his racing career eventually

caused a split between him and Sally. She gave birth to a child. Jimmy named the boy Jimmy Bryan Caruthers after his boyhood idol. Jimmy loved his young son, but the child was not enough to keep him and his wife together. In one sense the child was another anchor that threatened his ability to do what he wanted. Soon after the boy's birth, Jimmy and Sally separated.

Doug bought a new car for Jimmy in 1970. Bob Tattersall drove Jimmy's old car. That seemed to change Jimmy's luck. He ran the early season USAC races on the West Coast. Although winning none, he finished well in all and actually led in the point standings as the racers headed east for the summer season.

En route to the Midwest, Jimmy stopped in Phoenix, Arizona. While stationed in nearby Fort Wachutka, he had made many close friends. One of them was Jerry McClung, king of the local tracks around Phoenix.

Jimmy Caruthers convinced Jerry McClung to accompany him to Indianapolis, where they could find a rooming house, garage their cars together, and cut expenses. McClung agreed and obtained Ramada Inns as his sponsor, which meant they would never have to pay for motel rooms on the road. They also convinced McClung's mechanic, Jim Williams, that he should join in their adventure. They shared his expenses and each paid him fifty dollars a week. It was not the best financed team in racing, but that was the way you started if you had big ambitions.

Jimmy was a free spirit, a lover of life. He often acted on impulse. He still had not lost his boyish enthusiasm. He was not like some of the older drivers who, after so many years of facing death on the circuit, often become morose. Jimmy seemed never to take anything seriously. It was, at the same time, his greatest fault and his most endearing trait.

McClung, on the other hand, was more serious, trusting,

innocent, a bit naive, and as such often found himself target of his friend's practical jokes.

At Kokomo, Indiana, one night, Jimmy pocketed a water pistol when he climbed into his race car. The track remained wet from rain the previous night, so the drivers drove slowly at first, packing the track, getting it firm and in condition to race. Jimmy moved past Jerry's car, pulled the water pistol out of his pocket, and squirted his friend in the face.

Jerry seemed startled by the spray of water on his goggles. He failed to notice Jimmy pointing a water pistol at him. McClung nervously stared at his temperature gauge, tapping it to see if it worked.

Jimmy slowed, pulled his car around and behind McClung, and came up from the other side. He squirted his friend's windshield. McClung drove into the pits, ripped off his helmet, and started to climb out of his car. "We've got a leak in the cooling system," he told mechanic Jim Williams.

Suddenly Jimmy Caruthers rammed him from the back. *Whummp!* McClung turned around and saw Jimmy pointing the water pistol directly at him. *Squirt!* Jimmy let him have it right in the face.

Near the end of the season Jimmy and Dave Strickland (a veteran driver from Pleasant Hill, California) remained a few points apart in the battle for the USAC midget championship. In late August, the official schedule sandwiched one California race between two in the Midwest. Points could be scored at Santa Fe Speedway near Chicago Friday night, at Ascot Park near the Los Angeles airport Saturday night, and in Sun Prairie, Wisconsin, just west of Milwaukee, on Sunday. A California car owner promised Strickland a car should he come west to race, and Jimmy's father (who remained on the West Coast that summer) would supply one for his son, so neither had to worry about the near impossible task of transporting their midgets two thousand miles. They did have to worry about the cost of transporting themselves. The temptation for the two battling drivers to drive all three races was great, but the immediate financial rewards slight.

Before heading for the first race at Santa Fe, Caruthers and Strickland talked about whether or not they should make the long, expensive trip to California. "This is ridiculous," Strickland complained. "There is no way we can make money running all three of these races."

Jimmy nodded. "No way."

"Even if one of us goes out to Ascot and wins, he won't earn enough to pay his plane fare. There's no way we can survive trying tricks like that."

"No way."

"So look, I'll skip California if you do. That way neither of us gains any points."

Jimmy agreed.

Friday night at Santa Fe, Strickland won the feature event with Jimmy Caruthers finishing fifth. Strickland stopped at the finish line for the series of ceremonies that accompanied victory: presentation of the trophy, kissing the trophy girl, interviews on the public address system. Returning to the pits, he noticed Jimmy Caruthers' yellow pickup truck leaving the track. He thought that looked suspicious.

An hour later Strickland arrived at the departure gate at O'Hare Field in time to catch the 11 P.M. flight for Los Angeles. Sitting in the waiting room was Jimmy Caruthers. The two drivers burst out laughing.

Strickland won the race Saturday night in California, but Jimmy beat him in Wisconsin on Sunday. Their battle for the championship remained close, but at Du Quoin in September, Jimmy won both features at a two-event midget race, taking a commanding lead. He also earned $2000, his biggest payday of the season. After the race he stayed in the infield, signing autographs for the fans. Someone brought a bunch of watermelons down to the pits. He took a bite of watermelon, signed some autographs, ate more watermelon, signed more autographs.

As a boy, Jimmy Caruthers stood in the pits, watched winning drivers mobbed by fans, and dreamed of the day when it would happen to him. And now it was happening. He felt a strange euphoria rush through him, a feeling he never experienced before. Life was sweet, and he wished he could slap at some lever and shift it into low gear so he could relish the feeling even longer.

2

Rolling down the highway of life. The radio in his pick-up truck playing funky good music. The beer cold against his lips. The hum of the tires on the pavement. The rush of air past the window. One palm resting lightly, comfortably, on the steering wheel. Out of the way, world! I'm Jimmy Caruthers, and I'm leading in points.

Leading in points! Six months earlier he was ready to chuck it all—his whole racing career. Fresh out of the Army, driving a new machine, upside down more times than rightside up. Not one stinking victory during the entire previous season. He couldn't do anything right, not even piss straight in the men's room. Jimmy considered how close he had come to abandoning his boyhood dream of driving at Indy and shivered slightly. Nearly quit auto racing; quit the sport he loved. On the verge of becoming a respectable citizen, a man with strings, someone who reports to work at nine in the morning and quits at five that afternoon. *Whewww!*

Man, that was close, thought Jimmy. Anyone who survives in auto racing faces a number of crises—instances when he comes close to losing it, when a tire pops unexpectedly going into a corner, or an engine blows and dumps oil on the track, or he makes a damn-fool mistake and loses control. On those occasions maybe it is skill that saves the driver from careening into the wall, maybe it is luck, and sometimes it requires a little bit of both. Jimmy Caruthers almost lost it; and man, that was close.

Hey, Jimmy thought to himself, I was ready to *quit!* I mean, I'm no fool. I'm not going to hang around this sport forever just to prove my courage, to strut around the pits in my driver's uniform and look pretty for all the girls hanging on the fences. "Hey, Jimmy, sign my program!"

I don't want to be like some of those others—forty-five years old, never made the field at Indy, and still driving outlaw races out on the Coast. No way! If I can't be a winner in auto racing, I'll be a winner in something else, like building mobile homes.

Trouble is, you don't get your picture on the cover of *Sports Illustrated* for building mobile homes.

But losing was for last year, and Jimmy Caruthers of Anaheim, California, was leading in points! The car working better—or maybe being driven better. Finally getting the feel after those two years gone in the Army. Pitching the midget racer into the tight corners, the little monster clawing, biting, screaming, shrieking, bouncing. Like an unbroken bronco, like a rock rolling down the mountain, like a jackhammer programmed for destruction.

Instead of merely hanging on, he was exerting control: a flip of the wrist here, a slight pressure there, a tug, a pull, whatever it takes to keep the feisty machine and himself poised on the fine line between mediocrity and disaster. "Don't ask me how I do it. I just do it." His feet beat the pedals on the floor of his machine in staccato rhythm—

stomp on the brake, stand on the gas. An artist at his trade. A master of his profession.

And most important: *in control!* In control of his car. In control of his life.

Jimmy glanced to the right, where his traveling companion, Jerry McClung, sat, eyes closed but not asleep, thinking ahead down the highway, lost in his own thoughts, his own dreams, his own races to be run and won, his own visions of the future.

"Hey, McClung!"

"Shut up, Caruthers. I'm trying to sleep."

"I've got the world by the nuts!"

"Yeah, you once told me."

One traveler on the midget circuit during the summer of 1970 was Suzie Grim. Suzie's father was Bobby Grim, rookie of the year at Indianapolis in 1959. He competed ten times in the Indy 500 without ever coming close to winning. He was a good driver, but one who never quite got a first-class ride in a competitive car. Now, near the end of his career, Bobby drove midgets on the USAC circuit, hanging on, not quite ready to let go, still having a good time.

Bobby Grim usually traveled with his family, which included his wife, his son Bobby, Jr., and Suzie, who in 1970 was twenty years old and cute, with long brown hair.

Suzie attended Purdue University for a year, studying to become a teacher, but left the West Lafayette campus to work. She attended school part-time, worked part-time, and usually spent summer weekends traveling with her Dad to races.

Although Bobby Grim was not Suzie's real father, she carried his name. She had been born Suzan Lueptow in 1950, daughter of Frank Lueptow, who died two years after her birth in a stock car race in Atlanta. Bobby, a close friend of Frank, later began dating his widow. In 1954 they married. Suzie could not remember her real father, so Bobby Grim became the person she thought of as father.

Suzie grew up with racing an important part of her life. Her parents lived at the Georgetown Trailer Park, only a short distance from the Speedway, along with many racing families. They were part of the racing crowd, a somewhat clannish group of people who usually did things together because their interests were identical.

The Grims moved out of their trailer court in the sixties to a house, still within sight and hearing range of the famous racetrack. The largely residential area immediately west of the Indianapolis Motor Speedway is officially known as Speedway, Indiana. A suburb of Indianapolis, it exists almost as an island within that city. Living in Speedway, Indiana, is somewhat like living near the runway of a busy airport—at least during the month of May. Engines whine almost continuously, from nine in the morning until six at night, as drivers practice for the big race. Only when the engine noise stops do people on the west side look up from what they're doing, startled by the silence. "Oh my goodness," Suzie's mother used to say during these periods of frightening emptiness, "I wonder what happened."

The engine noise stops because the cars no longer are running. They stop when yellow lights flash on the track, signaling drivers to return to the pits. Sometimes it is because of rain. Sometimes it is because of oil or debris on the track. Sometimes because a driver loses control and spins into the wall.

Growing up in racing is a tragic way to grow up, thought Suzie, because you lose so many people you love. Her stepfather lost numerous friends—Judd Larson, Chuck Rodee, Don Branson. It seemed to Suzie like one friend after another was getting hurt, and she often became upset. But her interest in racing never faded.

Racing people often speak of those who get killed in

race cars as getting *hurt,* rather than dying. It is one of the euphemisms they use in dealing with death. Suzie Grim, at age twenty, had seen a lot of hurt in her days.

She had seen good times, too. Tragedy always comes mixed with good times, such as getting everybody together and driving up to Colfax, a tiny town forty miles north of Indianapolis where a restaurant featured the world's most delicious catfish. The Grims' circle of racing friends made pilgrimages to Colfax at least once during the month of May and once or twice more during the summer, usually a group of twenty or thirty people racing up to the town, eating, then racing back.

A member of their group named Carl Hungness had been eyeing Suzie during the summer of 1970, a fact not lost on either Suzie herself or Jimmy Caruthers. One time at Colfax Jimmy talked Suzie into teasing Carl. Suzie wore a jump suit that day featuring peek-a-boo slits in the side which Carl immediately noticed. Suzie leaned near Carl while they were eating dinner and commented, "My, isn't it cold in this restaurant?"

Carl agreed that it was, indeed, cold.

"It sure is," said Suzie. "See how cold my stomach is." She took Carl's hand and placed it through one of the peek-a-boo slits and onto her bare stomach.

Carl agreed that she had a very cold stomach. It was a shattering experience for him. Carl was about to reach for the ketchup bottle to pour ketchup on his catfish. Instead, he reached for his beer bottle by mistake. *Gush!* Beer all over his catfish. Jimmy Caruthers, watching the scene from the corner, doubled over with laughter. "No, Carl. You're supposed to take a bite of fish and *then* drink the beer."

Suzie could not recall first meeting Jimmy Caruthers. He was just someone who was around racing, had been around racing for quite a while. With or without a car,

Doug Caruthers usually showed up at the Speedway in May and often had his son, Jimmy, with him.

"Hi, Jimmy. When did you get in from California?"

"Just drifted in on the last breeze."

During the summers of 1969 and 1970, Suzie Grim traveled with her father to all the midget races. Since Jimmy was driving the circuit those years, too, they were members of the same traveling circus. If you heard Suzie and Jimmy talking, you never would suspect either of them liked each other. It was one insult after another. They were both young, cocky, and gave each other a hard time.

Jimmy would start: "I didn't know they accepted skinny girls in Purdue, Grim."

Suzie would reply: "I didn't know they allowed fat drivers in midget cars, Caruthers."

"Do you know the Golden Girl, Grim? I've always wanted to meet the Golden Girl."

"I understand the management plans to play your theme song before the feature event: the 'Beer Belly Polka.' "

"Your mother is such an attractive and pleasant lady. I wonder what happened when it came to you?"

"You have a unique style of driving a race car, Caruthers—upside down."

"If you want me to autograph your program, Grim, just let me know."

"If you need any help signing your name, Caruthers, just let me know."

"Well, I've been looking for someone to carry my helmet bag, Grim."

"Don't you have trouble finding helmets that fit your head, Caruthers?"

"No, I use an inflatable model."

"If you're talking about your head, Caruthers, I agree."

Suzie got revenge on Jimmy one time at Granite City. It

was one of those still, hot, humid, typically Midwest evenings. Tornado warnings were being broadcast on the radio. A number of drivers, Jimmy Caruthers included, came from California and knew very little about tornadoes and had never seen one. "Hey, Tat. What's a tornado look like?"

So Bob Tattersall of Streator, Illinois, attempted to give them a meteorology lesson. He pointed toward the southwest at a bunch of darkly menacing clouds. "Well, take those clouds up there."

"Yeah?"

"See how they're forming? A little tail comes out of the clouds and that's how tornadoes happen back here."

Jimmy squinted up at the clouds, as did the other West Coast drivers, still uncertain what to look for. "You mean like *that*?"

Tattersall stared where Jimmy was pointing and his jaw dropped. "Holy cats, that *is* a tornado!"

A black funnel cloud approached, its tail lazily twisting back and forth. The tornado seemed headed toward the racetrack, a real, wheel-banging, kicking tornado. Others spotted the tornado at that same time. Suddenly the infield and grandstands emptied as everybody rushed for their automobiles to get out of the tornado's path.

Everybody, that is, except Jerry McClung. He ran to his midget race car, strapped on his helmet, buckled his safety harness, and just waited.

"What the hell you doing, McClung?"

"You've got to have a survival plan!" Jerry shouted back. "What?"

"I figure a tornado can't flip me around any more than some of you wild drivers."

"You're crazy, McClung!"

The rain started. Then came hail. Lightning flashed. The roar was deafening, like a hundred midgets sliding out of turn one. Jimmy Caruthers and Carl Hungness, victim of the peek-a-boo dress caper, ran to Jimmy's pickup truck, parked outside the track. But when Jimmy tried to move, the truck stuck in the mud. He tried shifting—forward, reverse, forward—but the wheels spun. The truck sank lower and lower. At that moment Suzie Grim drove past in her automobile and saw their problems. Rolling down the window, she shouted, "Hey, Carl, want to go with me?"

So Carl climbed out of Jimmy's truck, ran to Suzie's car, and rode away with the girl, leaving Jimmy Caruthers stuck in the mud. Jimmy sat in his yellow pickup truck and nervously awaited the moment when he would be lifted up like Dorothy in *The Wizard of Oz* and be deposited who knows where. Sometimes at a racetrack you have to trust your life to fate.

The tornado never touched down. And Jerry McClung's survival plan went untested.

Suzie Grim worked evenings at Paul Harris' dress shop in the shopping center on Crawfordsville Road near the Speedway. Now and then Suzie looked up and saw Jimmy Caruthers walking by the store. She always gave him a friendly wave. He usually looked surprised at seeing her, as though he forgot she worked there. But he came in to say hello and chat.

"Hi, Suzie, what's doing?"

"Nothing much, Jim."

"Well, guess I'll head on my way."

"Glad you stopped by, Jim."

Only much later did Suzie discover that Jimmy Caruthers walked back and forth past the dress shop maybe nineteen times, waiting for her to look up and notice him.

Toward the end of the summer, when Jimmy won the midget race at Du Quoin, he received in the winner's circle a silver bowl filled with money. You don't earn much driving midgets, so the money consisted mostly of small bills.

Nevertheless, it looked like a fortune. At that stage of Jimmy Caruthers' career it was.

Walking back through the pits, four inches off the groud, chin up, eyes skyward, carrying the silver bowl with all that money before him in his two hands, he passed Suzie. He returned to ground momentarily. He smiled. She was smiling, too. "Great race," she said, and gave him a kiss.

"Thanks," He still held the silver bowl filled with money in both hands. He gave it to her.

"What's this for?"

"I'd give all of this for a date with you," he said, the wide grin still on his face.

Suzie laughed. She handed the bowl back and the crowd of well-wishers and autograph seekers swept him away from her. She assumed Jimmy was kidding in offering to trade the silver bowl for a date. Jimmy Caruthers always was kidding.

In September she learned he was not. One of the last big midget races in the Midwest is the "Hud One Hundred" in Terre Haute, Indiana. After that race the action shifts to Sacramento, San Jose, Phoenix. Jimmy arrived in Terre Haute still leading in points, his belongings packed, all of his gear in the back of his pickup truck, planning to continue to the West Coast for the winter. He hoped to stay in front of Dave Strickland and win his first USAC championship, but at Terre Haute, neither he nor Strickland did well. The championship would have to be settled in the late fall races on the West Coast.

That night, after the race, all the drivers attended a party featuring Mexican music. Everybody wore sombreros. After one of the dances Jimmy stood in the corner, talking to Suzie Grim.

"Hey, I really would like to take you out sometime," he said.

"Oh," she replied, not certain what to say. She still thought of Jimmy Caruthers as someone she knew while growing up. It's hard to think about becoming romantically involved with childhood friends.

Jimmy continued, "Well, would you consider going out with me if I ever asked?"

Suzie did not answer immediately. For a long moment she stared back at him, still pondering her reply.

"Well?" he said, breaking the silence.

Suzie's response came almost in a whisper. "I don't think so."

"Why not?"

"Mainly it's because I'm going steady with someone else."

"Yeah," agreed Jimmy Caruthers. He suddenly burst out laughing. "I guess that is a pretty sound reason."

The telephone rang at the Grim home in October. Suzie's mother indicated that the call was for her. "Who is it?" asked Suzie.

"It's Jimmy Caruthers," said her mother.

"Jimmy Caruthers?" Suzie took the telephone. "What are you doing back in town?" she said into the receiver.

"I'm not back in town," announced Jimmy. "I'm still in California."

"Oh?" Suzie seemed uncertain what to say.

"Listen," Jimmy began, "if I came back to Indianapolis next week, would you go out with me?"

She gazed over her shoulder to see if her mother was listening.

There was a long silence before Suzie answered. "You mean you'd travel all the way to Indianapolis to take me out?"

"Yeah!"

"I don't believe it."

"I would."

"You're crazy." He could not see it, but she was slowly shaking her head.

"I'm going to race midgets out east," admitted Jimmy. "Since I'm flying, I thought I'd make a quick stop in Indianapolis." Another long silence. "We could go to the movies."

"Which one?"

"How do I know? I'm not in Indianapolis."

Suzie thought for a moment. "I'm not sure."

"I'll buy you popcorn."

A smile crossed her face.

"With butter on it?"

"That's fifteen cents extra, but what the hell!"

"Maybe."

"Good. I'll give you a call when I hit town."

"I just said *maybe*," Suzie insisted, frowning. "I still want to decide whether—" But Jimmy had already hung up. Suzie stood with the receiver in her hand for what seemed like a very long time before replacing it on the cradle.

The following weekend, when Jimmy Caruthers passed through Indianapolis, he called Suzie Grim. They went to the drive-in on Lafayette Road.

3

Honk. Honk. "Hey McClung! Come out and play!" Jimmy Caruthers sat in his yellow pickup truck, engine still running, parked in the driveway beside Jerry McClung's house in Phoenix, Arizona. In the back of the truck was a motorcycle, also yellow.

McClung came to the garage door dressed in Jeans and T-shirt, sweating, rubbing his hands on an oily rag. "What you doing in town, Caruthers?"

"Got a race to run this weekend," Jimmy explained.

"You running that champ car race over at Phoenix International?"

"Someone's going to let me try their car."

"No bull!"

Jimmy grinned at him and nodded. "Get your bike. We're going riding in the desert."

Ten minutes later the two friends headed east down Base Line Road in Jimmy's pickup, two motorcycles now in the back. They were aimed at the open desert and the mountains beyond. When the road ended, they parked the truck, dropped its tailgate, and unloaded their motorcycles.

"What's out that way?" asked Jimmy, pointing east.

"Florence," McClung replied.

"You mean like Italy, with all those statues and churches?"

"Nope, just a bitty little Arizona town with cactus and adobe huts, and maybe a gas station or beer joint or two."

"Well, what are we waiting for?"

McClung and Caruthers hopped on their bikes and headed out onto the desert, across the crusty sand, kicking up rooster tails of dust in their wake, dodging clumps of adobe grass, an occasional gnarled tree, rocks, pebbles, cactus, a rusted beer can, some shotgun shells.

Jimmy aimed his motorcycle at the mountains, but it seemed that no matter how fast he drove, he could not approach them. After ten minutes of hard pounding, the mountains still seemed miles away. It was as though they were on rollers and some giant stood behind them, tugging on a rope and pulling the mountains away exactly as fast as he approached.

Jimmy turned his cycle into a dry wash and followed it, twisting and turning along what must have been the imprint of a river, if water ever ran in this dry wilderness. He continued along the wash until the going got too rough, then yanked his handlebars, pulled on the throttle, and shot up and out, heading toward the top of a small rise, the only thing resembling a hill in miles and miles of riding. He skidded his bike to a halt and cut the engine, listening for a moment to the *roar roar* of McClung coming up behind him. The second rider slid his cycle to a halt beside Jimmy and cut engine, too. There was a long period of silence, punctuated by the crackling of engines cooling and the heavy breathing of the riders. It was as though nobody dared talk. They sat on their cycles, straining their ears, listening for sounds: a cry of help, the rattle of a snake's tail, the croaking of an iguana, any sign of life in the surrounding wasteland. They heard nothing.

Caruthers finally broke the silence. "We're only ten miles away from a half million people, and it's like the middle of the Sahara."

"That it is," McClung agreed.

"There's something about getting away from people," Jimmy continued.

"Yeah."

"It makes me feel like I've got the world by the ass!"

Standing in the infield at the paved mile racetrack southwest of Phoenix, Jimmy Caruthers felt moisture forming in his armpits, trickling down the side of his body, staining his driver's uniform. It was a typically hot Arizona day in late fall, but not that hot. He was nervous.

A short distance away by the side of the track, the crew of the Thermo-King Special made final adjustments on the car driven by Gary Bettenhausen at Indianapolis earlier in the year. Jimmy was finally getting a chance to drive a championship car. Don Gerhardt, owner of the sleek blue racing machine, called earlier in the week to say he planned to enter a second car in the Phoenix 150, the last race on the championship trail. "Would you be interested in driving it?" It took Jimmy Caruthers approximately two tenths of a second to say yes.

Jimmy knew he received the call because he was young and was winning USAC's midget division. Maybe someone suggested that Gerhardt call; maybe Goodyear. The tire companies, with their budgets totaling hundreds of thousands of dollars, have a subtle way of affecting the lives and careers of drivers. He was being given a chance to demonstrate that his ability to drive midget cars could be translated into an ability to drive a championship car. Did he have the skill to win someday at Indianapolis? Someone wanted to know.

It did not always happen. Some great midget racers never seemed to make it in championship cars. Maybe because the latter cars were so fast, so expensive, and so finely tuned. Their handling characteristics were more subtle, more refined, and there was so much smaller a margin of error. Jimmy knew he had the ability to drive championship cars. He hoped he could convince others of that ability.

"Okay, Jimmy."

Jimmy glanced up to see Phil Casey, Gerhardt's mechanic, motioning toward him. The blue car was now ready to be taken out onto the track for practice laps before qualifying.

Jimmy dropped his cigarette to the concrete and crushed it underfoot. He walked to the side of the car and reached into the cockpit for the yellow helmet with "Jimmy Caruthers" written on it in script. Inside the helmet were his driving gloves. He took them out. He adjusted the helmet tightly on his head, buttoned the snaps, then pulled on the gloves. He stepped into the cockpit of the car, gingerly, as though not wishing to smudge it, and lowered himself as though into a bathtub.

He let himself slide forward far into the racing machine. His feet reached for the pedals far up in the nose of the finely crafted and meticulously polished championship car. The last person to drive this car had been taller than Jimmy, and several more adjustments needed to be made in the positioning of the pedals and the seat. He made a mental note to tell Casey this when he completed practice. Jimmy gripped the steering wheel, flexing his fingers to make sure they would do their job. He glanced into the rear-vision mirrors on each side of the car to make certain they were properly adjusted.

God, thought Jimmy Caruthers, this is a magnificent piece of machinery. Shiny. Polished. Well built. You slid into it, and if everything was going right between the two of you, there was no greater feeling on earth. It was impossible to describe adequately. When he was a boy, coming to the Speedway with his old man, he had been permitted on occasion, because of his father's connections, to climb into the cockpit of one or more of the cars that raced in the 500, and those experiences had been awe inspiring. This time, not only was he being permitted to sit in the car; he also would drive it.

Casey knelt by the side of the car, shouting instructions. He had to shout because Jimmy had his helmet on and plugs in his ears. With other drivers practicing on the track, the roar of their engines made conversation difficult. Mark Donohue. Mario Andretti. Bobby Unser. A. J. Foyt. And he, Jimmy Caruthers, was about to join them.

"Take it easy out there," Casey cautioned. "Just get the feel of the car first. You'll have time to work it up to speed later."

Jimmy nodded, and Casey rose and signaled for one of the other mechanics to shove the electric starter into the rear of the machine. Behind Jimmy was a $25,000 Offenhauser engine that would generate 600 horsepower and propel him at speeds over 150 miles per hour.

The starter whined. The engine caught with a raw, unmuffled roar. Jimmy could feel the vibrations running through him as the engine idled unevenly. He touched the throttle pedal and the engine sighed loudly, but smoothly. *Vroooom!* He massaged the pedal, letting the revolutions rise and fall. *Vroooomm! Vroooom!* This is it, he thought. *They're actually going to let me drive this thing!*

Casey signaled for him to move out onto the track. Jimmy eased up on the clutch, pushed gently on the throttle pedal, and it happened just the way they said it would. The race car inched forward down the pit runway. *It moves, damn it! It moves!* Jimmy was soaked with sweat, more from anticipation than from effort. As the car headed out of the pits he felt the gentle rush of air through the cockpit begin to cool him. He wanted to shout, to express his joy somehow, his excitement, his love for this great, wonderful piece of fine machinery wrapped around him. *This is what it's all about!*

He moved out onto the track now, still rolling at a slow pace. He glanced carefully into his rear-vision mirrors, making certain no faster cars were coming up from behind. He was a rookie, knew he was a rookie, and didn't want to make some dumb rookie mistake and get in the way of another driver. He remained low on the track, afraid to move up too soon into the groove, the fast lane, the area where the good drivers drove when they raced at full speed.

He knew where the groove was. He had asked other drivers about how to drive the Phoenix track. He watched them run here, at other races, and in previous years. He sat in the stands and analyzed what they did, thought of how he would do it when he got the chance. That morning he even climbed on his motorcycle and drove to the top of the hill overlooking the track and stared at it from above. It was as though someone had taken a crayon and drawn a dark line around the racetrack, reaching high on the first turn, then angling low on the backstretch until it almost reached the infield in the middle of the track's dogleg bend, moving wide again to hit the final turn at the proper angle, then out onto the main straightaway.

He knew the line. He could see it in his sleep. He knew where to drive. But knowing where to drive and being able to sit in the cockpit of a machine generating 600 horsepower and do it were two different things. He pressed steadily down on the throttle and felt the thrust of power shoving his hips forward. The car moved faster, faster, and as it did he eased himself up into the groove. Now he was racing, even if only with the stop watch. The infield spun past him, a blur in his side vision. The hill he stood on that morning formed another blur to the outside. Only the track ahead stayed in focus, a black ribbon, moving, dodging, trying to escape him, and he needed to keep his wheels planted firmly on that ribbon to survive.

He tried to be smooth, because he knew he needed to be smooth. Midgets were skittish machines that jumped and bounced all over the track, especially on dirt, and you had to react quickly, sometimes with brute strength to keep them pointed in the right direction. But championship cars were finely balanced, and brute strength did no good. Although he had been told to expect it, Jimmy was surprised at how little physical effort it took to drive this car in comparison with those he knew so far in his racing career. It took more finesse than strength, more skill than reaction. He tried to be gentle and smooth and kind to the car under his command, and hoped it would be gentle and smooth and kind to him.

The wind rushed past as he edged the car closer and closer to its maximum speed, and suddenly he was no longer sweating because he knew he could succeed. The harsh vibrations of the engine that jarred him so while sitting in the pits smoothed out, the explosive noise now no more harsh than the rush of the wind, a sound left far behind him as he rushed around the track at speeds in excess of a hundred miles per hour. He would be gentle, *so* gentle.

He felt he was running faster than anyone who ever drove this track before, but he knew this was not true. He probably was still running ten or fifteen miles per hour slower than what a veteran USAC driver might reach on the track in a top-class machine. If he needed any proof, it was there in his rear-vision mirror. While he circled the track at what seemed like breathtaking speed, another car, a blue and gold one, grew larger in his mirror as it closed the distance from behind. Jimmy did not need to study its reflection long to know it was Mark Donohue's car. Donohue had been turning the fastest laps that morning. As a rookie Jimmy knew he should get out of Donohue's way.

Suddenly Donohue was no longer in his rear-vision mirror, but was moving alongside him on the inside as the two cars came down the straightaway past the grandstand. They approached the first turn side-by-side, but with Donohue edging past. He had position and could now claim the fast line on the track. Jimmy would have to give way or crash, something he hardly wanted to do.

Jimmy moved over by a car width to give Donohue room. Then, not wanting to cause the more experienced driver any trouble, he moved over another half car width. He was out of the groove entirely as he came into the first turn, but with Donohue past him he would have time to get back into it. Maybe he could tuck in behind Donohue's tail and learn something about driving the track.

At that moment he began to float. That was the only way to describe it. He felt as though the gravitational pull of earth had released him. Where once his car darted around the racetrack, responding swiftly to the pressure of his fingers on the steering wheel, going the way he pointed it, its position stable like a train on a rail, it now began skidding sideways. The tail, with its huge doughnut-shaped wheels, began to slide out of control. Smoke rose from the tires as the friction from scraping sideways across the track raised their temperature. The shriek of the scraping rubber sounded louder than the engine now.

It was a gentle slide, not an abrupt, nasty, bumping one like you get in midgets when you go out of control, and Jimmy thought he could correct it easily. He spun the steering wheel in the opposite direction, but the front wheels slid sideways, too, and failed to grip. He hit the brakes, locking all four wheels, but the slide continued, with the car moving up the banking of the first turn toward the wall. The wall approached so slowly that for a moment Jimmy thought if he released his shoulder harnesses, he could lean out over the side of the car and push the wall away with his hand, like a boat approaching a dock. But, of course, such action was unthinkable because, regardless of what his senses told him, he knew he was moving at a speed close to eighty miles per hour.

Wooomph!

The car struck the outside retaining wall a glancing blow. It bounced from the wall and slid down the banking toward the infield. The impact stunned Jimmy momentarily, but he did not lose his sense of what was happening to him. He kept his foot jammed down on the brake pedal, afraid the car would have another spasm and spin up and into the wall again. It did not, and instead slid gently to a halt in the infield, raising an enormous cloud of dust that momentarily obscured his vision.

The first thing Jimmy thought about after the car came to a halt was fire. All drivers fear fire, and he was no exception. He hit the release button on his shoulder harness and placed his palms on the sides of the cockpit to push himself out of it. As he did this, he felt someone's hands lifting him by the armpits. They sure get to you fast, he thought. He jumped free of the car and moved quickly away, but there was no fire.

He was unhurt, or seemed unhurt. He felt his body as though to prove he was all there, that he had not left some parts behind. The collision with the wall had been barely enough to stun him. But as the dust clouds settled and he returned his attention to the car, he felt he would get sick. The once beautiful, brightly polished championship car with its gleaming parts had been defiled. The right rear wheel was badly bent. The rear wing had been half torn off. There were ugly scrapes and dents.

Gerhardt's pit crew ran up and he saw they were looking at the race car—not at him. They didn't care about him; it was their race car they worried about. He was just another dumb driver—a *chauffeur*—who could be replaced if necessary. They could walk back into the pits and find a half dozen other drivers ready to jump into anything they produced with four wheels and an engine. Their race car, on the other hand, could be replaced only by long hours of work, hours that would be paid for without the time-and-a-half extra pay that one normally gets in a factory job. He was adding to their work schedule and for that they could be expected to dislike him. Drivers were the enemies of mechanics because they kept tearing up their race cars.

Phil Casey did not seem that angry. "What happened?" he asked.

Jimmy laughed nervously. "I was trying to get out of Donohue's way," he alibied. "I wasn't going that fast."

"There's a lot of sand on the track," Casey commented. He said it coldly.

"Yeah."

"It wasn't entirely your fault."

"Thanks," said Jimmy. He frowned.

But as Jimmy walked back toward the pits alone, that word, *entirely,* bothered him. It wasn't entirely his fault. He knew that whether they said it or not, he messed up. He made a dumb rookie mistake. There was a lot of sand on the Phoenix racetrack, and being a dumb rookie, he was not expected to know that. So he messed up. If lightning came down from the skies, demolishing his car, he still would have messed up. If it had not been some dumb rookie in the car, he would have known enough to get out of the way of the lightning, and that was why you did not hire dumb rookies to drive your race cars, if you could possibly avoid it. Unless Goodyear tells you to give him a chance, and then they all pay the bill, sooner or later, for the damage done. Jimmy knew that as for driving Gerhardt's car anymore, or maybe any other car for a damned long while, he could forget it. Don't call us, dumb rookie. We'll call you.

"Gee whiz," said Jimmy Caruthers softly, unemotionally, almost as though to himself. He walked a few more steps toward the pits. "Gee whiz," he repeated. He said it without outrage, without passion. He said it because it was what you said after you messed up.

Jimmy wanted to scream. He wanted to cry. He wanted to take the helmet he was carrying in his hand—the one with "Jimmy Caruthers" written on it in script—and hurl it against the ground as hard as possible to demonstrate his disgust. He decided against doing it, however. It would not look cool.

There were better days and better nights. One of them came on November 26, Thanksgiving night, "Turkey night," as it was called, the Grand Prix, the last big USAC midget race of the season at Ascot Park in Gardena, California.

What happened in Phoenix earlier that month no longer mattered. This was a form of racing where Jimmy Caruthers excelled. He was the veteran, still battling Dave Strickland for the USAC title. Jimmy only finished fifth, but with his previously earned points this was good enough to assure himself the championship. Jimmy scored 409.70 points in USAC's complex system, and Dave Strickland was second with 397.22.

After the race the two shook hands. "You're a hell of a man," Jimmy told Strickland. "It wasn't me that beat you. It was the race car." He referred to the superiority of his new Sesco engine compared to the outdated Offenhauser Strickland used. Whether true or not, Dave Strickland would remember Jimmy's comment long after he forgot the disappointment of finishing second.

The next morning Jimmy called several of his friends in Indianapolis to let them know about his winning the championship. He spoke to Suzie Grim's mother; Suzie was at work. "Suzie is engaged to be married," explained Mrs. Grim.

"She's what?" asked Jimmy, suddenly surprised.

Mrs. Grim confided that her daughter recently became engaged, that she and her husband did not particularly like their prospective son-in-law, whom Suzie knew from high school. The boy was someone outside the racing crowd. "She's only doing it because all her friends are getting married."

"That's a dumb reason."

"Well, Suzie is twenty," sighed Mrs. Grim. "She's afraid of being an old maid."

"She's nuts."

"If you think so, why don't you tell her?"

Jimmy called Paul Harris' dress shop and asked for Suzie Grim. It was their first conversation since going to the drive-in in October. "I hear you're getting married," he began, trying to sound very matter-of-fact about the matter but not succeeding.

"I'm thinking about it," Suzie admitted.

"What do you mean, 'thinking about it?' "

"Well, maybe I'll change my mind."

"Don't let me discourage you," snapped Jimmy, his voice rising in pitch now. "I mean, if you want to ruin your life by marrying some dull clod that you don't love anyhow, be my guest."

"You're right, I don't love him."

"Then isn't it silly to get married?"

Afterwards, Suzie Grim broke the engagement, although not entirely, she claimed, because of Jimmy Caruthers, who after all made no promises to her.

At the USAC awards banquet in January, Jimmy collected two championship rings, two plaques for the wall of his trophy room, and a lot of applause for having won the midget championship. At twenty-five he became the youngest driver to achieve that honor. Somehow, receiving the award seemed less fun than the actual achievement.

Afterward, one of the race fans attending the banquet approached Jimmy and shook his hand, saying, "Jimmy, you're a real wheel banger."

Jimmy got a big grin on his face and his eyes twinkled, as though he knew a secret no one else knew. "Wait until you meet my kid brother!"

4

Until that time Jimmy Caruthers' kid brother, Danny, raced only on the West Coast. Eldon Daniel Caruthers was born on March 12, 1950, played football in high school, but, like his older brother, loved auto racing. He was nicknamed "Kid" Caruthers, and drove with that written on the side of his cars.

Danny first sat in a quarter midget at the age of three and a half. Later he drove three-quarter midgets on one of the so-called "outlaw" circuits—the United States Racing Club. He attended Fullerton Junior College to study auto mechanics, as had Jimmy before him. Like his older brother, he quit college after a year to race full-time.

That made Jimmy angry. "Goddam it, Kid. You ought to stay in college and get a decent education."

"You quit college, didn't you?" Danny argued. That made Jimmy even more angry, but it also shut him up. Jimmy Caruthers thought everybody else should get lots of education. He just was not that interested in college himself.

Bob Tattersall, who ran Doug Caruthers' second car in 1970, was sick and unable to drive the last race of the USAC season, Turkey Night at Ascot Park, so Doug let Danny drive Tattersall's car. It was Danny's first USAC race.

Danny was eager, too eager. Midway through the feature event, with Jimmy ahead of him and Dave Strickland behind, Danny edged wide going through the turn, hoping to put Strickland up in the dirt near the fence and slow him enough so his brother could win the championship. The more experienced Strickland simply hit the brake and slid beneath Danny, passing him.

After the race Jimmy and Dave laughed about Danny's foolish action. "The kid better be careful," Jimmy admitted, "or he'll be barred for life before he's started."

Later, Doug told Jimmy he planned to let Danny drive Tattersall's car during the 1971 season. Jimmy was surprised. "What about Tat?" he asked. "Who's he going to drive for?"

"Tattersall's not going to be driving," Doug explained. "He's sicker than we thought."

"What's wrong with him?"

"He's got cancer."

"Jesus Christ!"

Doug explained that doctors had found a malignant tumor in one of Bob Tattersall's kidneys. It had to be removed.

Jimmy shook his head slowly, amazed that the driver he raced with all summer could have something as serious as cancer eating away at him. "That's fatal, isn't it?" he asked.

"Not if you catch it in time," Doug responded.

Jimmy lapsed into silence. He was trying to remember how Bob Tattersall looked the last time they met, whether he seemed sick or not. He could not recall the other driver acting any different than before. Well, come to think of it, Tat did look tired toward the end of the season. But then, everybody looked tired toward the end of the season.

The thing that gave Jimmy pause was that Tat was so young, a man in his mid-thirties with most of his life seemingly still ahead of him. Jimmy expected some of his friends to get hurt in crashes. That was part of racing. You did not like it, but you accepted it. Being threatened by cancer was something outside the rule books.

"It's going to be tough on Tat," Jimmy mused, "not being able to drive this coming season."

Jimmy and Danny Caruthers were about as opposite as two men could be and still be brothers—in their looks, personalities, and racing styles.

Jimmy was short, muscular, and had long, curly, light brown hair. Danny was tall, lean, and had short, straight black hair. Jimmy, the complete practical joker, possessed an outgoing personality. Danny seemed much more of an introvert. Suzie Grim said of Danny: "He was the type of person who, if a bird fell out of a tree, would bend over and put it back in its nest." She considered him kind and gentle, although a bit immature.

Both brothers loved racing, but whereas Jimmy's off-track interests broadened to include motorcycling, flying, water skiing, and many other activities, Danny seemed totally preoccupied with auto racing to the point where some of the other drivers claimed they could not carry on a conversation with him about any other subject.

On the track Jimmy and Danny's personalities reversed. When he climbed into the cockpit of a racing machine, outgoing, fun-loving Jimmy Caruthers sobered suddenly. It was not that he became conservative—a tag he would strongly resent—but he showed reliability, polish, experience, and extreme safety consciousness. He was what others in the circuit described as smooth and steady and run hard all day.

These same drivers considered Danny brave to the point of being flashy. They felt he needed to be watched on a racetrack. He often drove way over his head. Most experts who watched both drivers race, however, thought Danny would rise to the top faster than had Jimmy.

Jimmy was more mechanically inclined, willing to try tricks such as the bypass valve he installed so that when his midget slowed under yellow flag conditions, the fuel would not foul the injection system. When the green flag dropped, he could get a jump on the field. Danny scoffed at such gimmickry: "Ah, I'll pass everybody next lap anyway."

The experts talked about Danny's tremendous talent, his natural ability, although talent and natural ability are difficult to identify in the auto sport in which so much depends on equipment. Jimmy insisted: "Hell, it's not talent pushing Danny. It's his fantastic desire!"

Jimmy possessed considerable desire himself. In a heat race at San Jose in February Jimmy came rushing through the pack from a rear starting position to take the lead. Danny battled Dave Strickland for second. Their father, standing near the first turn, signaled Jimmy that he had a long lead, that he should use all the racetrack. Doug neglected to inform Jimmy that Danny and Dave Strickland had moved to a position right on his tail.

After Jimmy took the checkered flag, he glanced over his shoulder and realized how close the two other drivers had been. He drove into the pits and snapped at his father, "You wanted Danny to win!"

"I was afraid if you knew he was there," alibied Doug, "you might ease up."

"Oh, come on, Pop."

"Strickland might have blown both of you off."

Jimmy said no more, but refused to allow Doug to give

47

him signals the rest of the season. He was very precise about how information should be relayed to him at the racetrack. Once Carl Hungness was signaling Jimmy during a forty-lap race in which Jimmy had a massive lead. On the thirty-ninth lap, as Jimmy received the white flag indicating one to go, Hungness abandoned his post at turn one and strolled back to the pits to await Jimmy's return. When Jimmy climbed out of his race car, he barked at Hungness, "Where the hell were you that last lap?"

"You had the race won," insisted Hungness.

"When I didn't see you there, it broke my concentration. I could have crashed. If you're going to do something, you do it right—or not at all!"

One night at Ascot Park Jimmy was working on his car following a heat race when he looked up and saw someone watching him. The person had a dark complexion and long black hair. He leaned on crutches, one leg in a cast. Jimmy thought the person looked familiar. "Aren't you Gene Romero?"

"How did you know that?" asked the man on crutches.

"Saw you wipe out here a couple of weeks ago."

"Don't remind me," the man on crutches winced.

Gene Romero was a motorcycle racer, better known to the fans by his nickname, "Burritto." He grew up in San Luis Obispo and began racing cycles with the American Motorcycle Association while still in his teens. He soon became one of the top bike riders on the circuit.

Motorcycle racing is a tough, dangerous sport. Unlike midget racers, who have seat harnesses and roll cages, motorcycle racers have little for protection other than a crash helmet and leather uniforms. In the pits motorcycle racers always walk with a limp because they wear heavy metal plates on their left feet, which are dragged straight-legged on the ground while sliding around dirt-track turns.

Jimmy Caruthers loved motorcycles, attended motorcycle races frequently, and admired the men who drove in them. After Gene Romero's first visit to the pits at Ascot, he and Jimmy became friends. Jimmy wanted to talk about motorcycles all the time, but discovered that Burritto would rather talk automobiles to him. Burritto hoped someday to graduate from two-wheeled racing into four-wheeled racing as a former AMA champion, Joe Leonard, once did. Jimmy often asked Burritto to come riding with him back in the near-wilderness hills that are part of the landscape around Los Angeles. "Let's go cow-trailing this afternoon," Jimmy suggested.

Burritto usually demurred. "I ride motorcycles for a living," he explained. "I don't do it for fun."

Because of their mutual interest in each other's profession, Gene Romero and Jimmy Caruthers grew closer. In 1970 Burritto won the AMA Grand National championship, earning the right to race with the number one on his cycle the following season. Jimmy won the USAC Midget Car championship the same year, so he, too, raced with the number one. Both enjoyed the notoriety and fame that came with their championships. They ordered business cards printed, identifying themselves as "number one."

On one occasion Jimmy and Burritto flew into a large city to rent a car. Burritto looked down the airport corridor at the series of car rental counters. "Well, which is it? Hertz or Avis?"

"Are you out of your skull?" snorted Caruthers.

"What's wrong?"

"It's Hertz! None of that number two junk for me!"

Jimmy and Gene Romero both spent a lot of time on the road away from home. They often raced on weekends hundreds of miles apart. They called each other long distance to find out how they did. When the schedule permitted, Jimmy attended Burritto's motorcycle races and Burritto attended Jimmy's automobile races. Their friendship soon became a bridge where many of the motorcycle and automobile racers, strangers though in allied businesses, came to know each other.

At first Doug Caruthers distrusted Gene Romero, afraid Burritto would make his son ride motorcycles and get hurt, and be unable to drive Doug's race car. Actually Burritto kept telling Jimmy, "Don't ride bikes on the streets. Ride them in the dirt, where it's safer."

Like Jimmy Caruthers, Gene Romero recognized the dangers of his profession. He respected his own ability as a motorcycle racer—just as he respected his friend's ability to drive automobiles—but he knew that skill and ability often were not enough. "Those fluke deals happen once in a while," Burritto once conceded to an interviewer, "where you're bending into a nice hundred-fifty-mph corner, and the engine locks up and pitches you right into the Armco barrier—and you are gone.

"The way our bikes are running on the superspeedways, people can get snuffed too easily. There are a lot of guys I've known who are dead. You never know when your time is up. Just like a stereo tape. When it comes to the end, the music's over."

Burritto continued, "In this kind of racket, you don't know what's going to happen; so you live for today. On the other hand, if you make it through the whole deal, then you better have something tucked away for the future."

Burritto knew his own abilities, and he also analyzed the abilities of his close friend: "You get a feeling for people, and whenever Jimmy races he races hard, but it seems like he always has his car under control. It isn't going to be some dumb thing that gets him, something where he screws up. He knows what he can do and what he can't do. If anything gets him, it will be one of those fluke deals where all of a sudden a part breaks, or there's a multi-car pile-up and there's no way to get through."

Racers don't dwell upon death. Only in rare moments of introspection do they admit that maybe they might not survive to the checkered flag.

In May Jimmy and Danny Caruthers threw their gear into the back of the pickup and headed east for the summer midget season. They towed their midgets behind them in a new trailer that they dubbed "the yellow submarine." Before they came east, Danny asked his brother, "Could you talk to Goodyear about getting me a new driver's uniform?"

Jimmy laughed, "You ain't leading in points, Kid. As soon as you are, start thinking about getting a new uniform."

Danny won his first race in Lima, Ohio. He won again the following weekend in DeGraff, Ohio, and then won races the following month in Springfield, Illinois, and Cincinnati. When not winning, he finished near the front. Soon he had the points lead. "What about that new uniform?" he asked Jimmy again.

"Now you can start *thinking* about it, Kid," laughed his brother.

Jimmy Caruthers knew the climb to the top in auto racing was long, arduous, and fraught with perils, not all of them on the track. More drivers want rides than there are cars available. Only thirty-three cars make the starting field at Indianapolis each year. Fewer than one third of them have any chance of winning the race. The pyramid in auto racing is broad at the base, narrow at the top. Jimmy enjoyed midget racing, but saw it as an interim step to driving in the Indianapolis 500. He still raced the little cars, but a second title did not motivate him. Several times during the season, when Danny's car was being repaired after a collision, Jimmy unselfishly loaned him his so Danny could earn more points toward the midget title. If a tire company offered Jimmy a new, improved tire, it often wound up on Danny's car. Jimmy had raised his sights higher—to the championship division.

In May Jimmy Caruthers spent most of his time at the Indianapolis Motor Speedway hoping someone would give him a chance to qualify for the 500. A lot of Jimmy's hope focused on Clint Brawner, a veteran mechanic who made his home off-season in Phoenix, Arizona. Brawner was considered one of the top wrenches at the Speedway. Among the drivers who once raced for Clint were Jimmy Bryan, A. J. Foyt, Roger McCluskey, and Mario Andretti. Brawner discovered Andretti driving a sprint car and gave him his first ride at Indy. The two recently split, and Brawner was reportedly scouting for another talented young driver like Mario.

Jimmy's father's friendship with Brawner dated back to the early fifties, before either arrived at the Speedway. Yet Doug wasted no time bragging to Brawner about his son's abilities. He knew Clint cared little for conversation. "You can't walk up and tell Clint someone's a good race driver," Doug explained to his son, "because he won't believe you. He has to see for himself."

Jimmy relayed Doug's comment later to Suzie Grim. "Why don't you try walking past his garage eighteen times?" she teased him. "Maybe he'll look up and notice you."

Jimmy laughed, "That only works with girls."

One night Brawner watched Jimmy drive at Indianapolis Raceway Park, a track located in Clermont, ten miles west of the Speedway. Clint commented afterwards to Doug, "He's smooth on pavement." For Clint Brawner, that was the ultimate compliment, a ringing gold medal endorsement. It meant he thought Jimmy Caruthers might move from midgets to championship cars, something not all drivers could do.

Brawner, however, was committed in 1971 to running with Art Pollard, and could offer Jimmy little more than encouragement. Pollard, a man in his forties, was one of the Speedway's oldest active drivers, although he had only driven at Indianapolis for a half dozen years. For most of his career he worked as a service manager for a Chevrolet dealer in Medford, Oregon, and raced mostly as a hobby in local events in the Pacific Northwest. A wealthy race fan finally built him a competitive stock car, which he drove on NASCAR's circuit on the West Coast. He achieved sufficient success so that he obtained a ride at Indianapolis in 1966. Two years later Andy Granatelli of STP offered him a ride in one of the revolutionary turbine cars. Joe Leonard and he came close to winning the race, but broken valves stalled their cars almost within sight of the finish line.

Pollard, easygoing, popular, never seemed to get angry. He rarely engaged in the wild pranks some drivers delighted in. He did not spend an excessive amount of time drinking in bars. He believed in physical fitness and worked out regularly with weights. When Art donned his driver's uniform and helmet, ready to climb into his race car, he joked, "I'm going to the office." He considered racing his business, although he seemed to derive more fun out of it than most drivers, many of whom were bothered by the tension.

Pollard reached the peak of his profession too late in life to be truly successful, but he was considered a dependable performer. Even though he might not squeeze an extra mile or two per hour out of a racing machine, he at least could be trusted to keep it between the walls. He won the Ontario 500 in 1970 by the simple expedient of staying on the track longer than a number of other drivers in faster cars who suffered mechanical failures. Sometimes victory goes to he who survives.

But in May at Indy it appeared as though Art Pollard

might have trouble even making the field. After Brawner split with Andretti, he designed a new car called Scorpion, but it never worked right. Pollard qualified on the first weekend, but with a slow time.

Early in the month George Snider practiced in Pollard's backup car, but disliked its handling characteristics and switched to another team. Brawner, searching the Speedway for a replacement, found young Jimmy Caruthers nervously smoking cigarettes, drinking coffee, hanging around the pits, looking for someone willing to offer him a chance.

"Caruthers, how would you like a ride?"

"Uh, yeah, Clint. I might be willing to give it a try."

Jimmy's response to Brawner was quick, matter-of-fact, almost curt: as though to say, *If you don't offer me the ride, Clint, someone else will, and it will be a better car!* Whether subconscious or not, Jimmy recognized the façade of bravado displayed by the men who race at Indianapolis. It was a confidence, almost an indifference to others, as well as themselves, that they all had to possess, or they would not succeed. It was a studied arrogance, an imperious attitude, which if not there to begin with was soon acquired. And within a fraction of a second, Jimmy Caruthers slipped easily from the role of worried outsider to that of haughty insider. "I might be willing to give it a try," he had said, and the casualness of his response shocked even Jimmy.

Yet he could not kid himself long, because the moment Clint approached him with the offer of a ride in the Indy 500, a chill cascaded down Jimmy's spine. This was the moment he dreamed of as a kid. Even more, he was getting another chance. After messing up once at Phoenix, he was getting another chance. A lot of drivers fail to get even *one* chance, much less two. As Jimmy walked with Brawner back to the garage in Gasoline Alley where the race car awaited him, Jimmy's chin tilted ever so slightly upward, his eyes gazed unfocused at the sky. Brawner was walking at his side talking animatedly about what Jimmy would need to do to qualify, but the words might as well have been hurled on a rocket into space. Jimmy's blood was churning. His pulse was quickening. That chill he felt was still there too. He was looking beyond the ride he was being offered by Brawner to the day he would stand in the victory circle acclaimed as the winner of the Indianapolis 500. This was what life was all about.

Before being permitted to qualify, rookie drivers at Indianapolis must demonstrate their competence by driving at varying speeds under the watchful eyes of veteran officials and other drivers. Jimmy took his rookie test the week between the two qualification weekends and passed without problems. But he never got a chance to qualify. Pollard was bumped from the field of thirty-three on Saturday by a faster car and had to use his backup car to requalify. Jimmy moved from the ranks of haughty insiders to nervous outsiders again. He watched the 500 from the grandstand.

The following weekend he was back on the inside again. He drove Pollard's backup car in Milwaukee. He placed twelfth. He drove the car again in the Pocono 500 and took thirteenth. Brawner took only one car to the Ontario 500 in California in September, but Bob Gerhardt let Jimmy drive his Thermo-King Special again. He finished nineteenth. Jimmy Caruthers did not yet have reporters buzzing around his pits, hailing him as the new Andretti, but he was beginning to establish a reputation as one who could be trusted to handle a championship car.

He found the breed different to drive than midgets. There were several reasons, many of them obvious to the fans. Championship cars had rear engines; midgets had engines in front. Drivers in championship cars reclined almost on their backs; midget drivers sat upright.

But there were other, more subtle differences, most of them related to handling characteristics, that only a driver could appreciate. The ragged line on which race drivers must run in order to succeed proved to be much finer in championship cars than in midgets. There was less margin for error—*much* less margin for error. "If you drive a midget too deep in the corner," Jimmy explained to Suzie, "you can throw the car into a slide and still stay between the fences. Make that same mistake in a championship car and it will spin." At racing speeds (200 mph plus down the straightaway at Indianapolis) a championship car will spin not once, but several times—if nothing gets in the way. The impact of a crash usually is severe. Race cars costing up to $100,000 can be destroyed simply because of a seemingly minor miscalculation on the driver's part. Sometimes the driver is destroyed with the car.

The threat of death did not seem to worry Danny Caruthers. He never considered it in his rush to glory. He did not seem willing to wait several years—as had his older brother—to make his presence felt. As the summer continued, he astounded race fans both with his driving techniques and his derring-do. In July the Caruthers brothers traveled to Springfield, Illinois, for a midget race at a quarter-mile dirt track. Danny won an earlier midget event on the same track in June, so considered himself a veteran. He drove recklessly, skidding so high through the turns that he bounced the rear off the fence each lap.

This infuriated Jimmy, who felt his brother courted danger with such wild driving stunts. Coasting into the pits after the feature event, he decided to tell Danny to quit driving like a madman before he killed himself, or someone else. Jimmy, however, could not get near his young brother because of the circle of fans surrounding Danny.

"Great race, Kid!"

"You really stand on the gas!"

"You're unbeatable!"

Jimmy abandoned his plan to lecture Danny that night and returned to his pickup truck. He complained to Suzie Grim: "How the hell do you tell a kid he's wild when the race fans tell him he's terrific?"

Danny got upside-down several times that season, the worst wreck at a race in Bloomington, New Jersey. But he walked away from that accident as well as others. He seemed to bear a charmed life.

Jimmy and Danny continued to dominate the midget circuit. During the year they set forty-seven new track records, won twenty out of fifty-two USAC feature events entered, and earned $38,000—a considerable sum to earn driving midgets. On six occasions the brothers finished first and second.

Toward the end of the season Danny began to drive more smoothly. He seemed less wild, took fewer chances. Instead of driving over people, he now drove around them. When he won still another feature event in Denver, Colorado, in September, Danny Caruthers held such a massive lead over the rest of the USAC midget field that he seemed certain to succeed his brother as champion. If so, he would become, at age twenty-one, the youngest midget champion in USAC history, also succeeding his brother for that honor. Even though Jimmy competed in a dozen fewer events than Danny, he held second place in the standings ahead of Dave Strickland and Jerry McClung.

But it had been a long, hard season with too many races, too much travel, endless nights working on the cars past midnight, then up early in the morning to travel to another town, another motel, strange beds, meals caught on the fly, never any time to relax. Everybody was beginning to get a bit tired of each other. Nerves were frayed. Tempers flared often. Even the joy of winning could not overcome the crushing effect of cumulative fatigue. Doug, particularly, seemed to be in a constant rage at the racetrack over one insignificant matter after another. At a race in Colorado Springs, Doug exploded at Jim Williams for what seemed like the twentieth time in two days, and the mechanic exploded back, "Slugger, I'm not going to listen to your bullshit one second longer!"

"Goddam it, Williams. You're fired!"

"Shit I am!"

"Shit you're not!"

Everybody, Jim Williams included, knew that Doug's temper expressed itself in flash fires rather than smoldering embers. His tantrums rarely lasted past the next race, and Williams could expect forgiveness before the end of the evening. No apology, but at least peace would return to the Caruthers pits. Jimmy never became involved in such battles. He detested conflict and avoided it as much as possible.

But it had been a long, hard season and Williams decided there was no reason for it to be any longer or harder. He decided to return to his home in Tempe, Arizona. He packed his bags and left the track before Doug had a chance to rehire him.

Afterwards, Doug seemed temporarily subdued by the incident. He recognized he was not an easy person to get along with at a racetrack. "My biggest problem," he admitted to Jimmy, "is I think we have to win every race."

Doug quickly forgot what happened. The split, however, deeply disturbed Danny Caruthers. He and Jim Williams had become close friends during their season together. Danny believed he owed his lead in the point standings as much to Williams' skill with a wrench as to his own bravado as a driver. No driver succeeds without good machinery, although not all acknowledge that fact.

Danny's anger simmered for a week until they reached Sacramento, California. Danny wanted the chassis of his midget set a certain way; Doug wanted a different setting. Doug knew from past experience his setting would work better on that particular track surface. He did not take time to explain fully his reasons. "Just drive the car," he told Danny, "and leave the thinking to me."

Danny's face turned brick red. He exploded, "I can get a ride with any other owner on the circuit, and he wouldn't give me half the grief I get from you."

"He wouldn't give you half as good a ride either," snapped Doug.

"There are plenty other good rides!"

"If you think so, go get one of them!"

The instant he made that remark, Doug regretted it. But Doug Caruthers was bull-headed. He had not earned his nickname, "Slugger," for nothing. He did not know how to back down gracefully. And Danny inherited that characteristic from him. Danny walked over to the grandstand and sat down. He did not race that evening. Doug eventually asked Gary Bettenhausen to drive his car.

The following day Danny contacted Jack Fitzpatrick, a car owner from Newport Beach who entered his midget mostly in West Coast races. Danny once flipped a car belonging to Fitzpatrick and figured he owed him a favor. "I'm available," he said.

"You've got a ride," Fitzpatrick replied, eager to have the USAC points leader sitting in his race car.

Jimmy tried to convince Danny not to leave their father. "We've got a winning combination. Why change?"

Although Danny's anger cooled considerably, he still stood by his decision. "Maybe I'll be back," he admitted, "but I don't want Pops to take me for granted."

On October 22 in Phoenix, Gary Bettenhausen finished first in Danny's car with Danny second in Fitzpatrick's car.

That increased Danny's total to 398.76 points and assured him (with only three races remaining on the USAC calendar) that nobody could overtake him for the championship. He saw Jim Williams at the track. The two talked about forming their own team for the following season.

He also promised his father he would drive for him on Turkey Night, the final event of the midget season. Before then, he planned to drive at least one more time for Jack Fitzpatrick at the Corona Raceway near Riverside, California.

On October 30 in Corona, the evening of racing began with practice, then qualifying—each driver going two fast laps against time to determine his position in four separate heats. Danny won one of the heat races, setting a new track record. Then there was a short trophy dash and a semi-event by which some of the slower cars might still move into the feature event. Before that final race the drivers waited in the pits, ready to take several additional practice laps to warm their cars—what is known as hot-lapping. Danny appeared anxious to get out on the track. He had his lap safety belt fastened securely, but had not yet attached his shoulder harnesses.

Danny Caruthers usually hot-lapped with his shoulder harnesses loose, even though Doug often warned him against this potentially dangerous practice. Danny ignored his father's advice because he liked to tinker with the "weight-jacker," the device which permitted him to adjust the chassis, while driving, to track conditions. Since it was positioned forward in the cockpit and difficult to reach, he left his shoulder harnesses unfastened to make adjustments more easily.

The Fitzpatrick midget was similar to the one he drove for his father, but minor differences did exist. One such minor difference involved the "kill" button. Midgets do

not have ignition switches, so the kill button is used at the
end of a race to cut the engine. On Danny's old car, the kill
button was located on the steering wheel; on Fitzpatrick's
car, the kill button was on the left side of the dashboard.

Before the feature event Doug Caruthers stood beside
his two midget cars. His son, Jimmy, sat in the number one
car he drove all season; Gary Bettenhausen occupied the
number five car, driven previously by Danny. The starter
signaled for the hot-lapping to begin. As Jimmy and Gary
rolled onto the track, Doug returned to his truck to secure
his tools.

Doug heard the rumble of well-tuned machinery, a
sound like music to his ears. To someone not used to the
cacophony of auto racing, midget cars produce constant
noise, a piercing, ear-splitting, sense-dulling roar. Doug
Caruthers, however, knew and understood this roar. Just
as a music lover can pick out the individual sounds of in-
struments in a symphony orchestra, he could hear the
sound of each race car being propelled around the track.
He knew which of those sounds were made by his cars. He
recognized the pitch of the engine in Jimmy's number one
car as well as that of the engine in the number five car. He
had good ears for racing sounds.

Coming down the straightaway, each driver stood on the
gas, the small but powerful engine under the hood of his
car winding up to near maximum revolutions. As he
reached the turn, he hit the brakes with one foot, releasing
the throttle with the other. The sound level coming from
that car's engine dropped, but only for an instant. Almost
immediately the driver stood on the gas again, released the
brakes, and powered through the turn, emerging on the
next straightaway, his engine straining once more to reach
maximum revolutions. If the driver slammed on the
brakes too hard, or failed to step on the throttle soon
enough, or made any one of a dozen other minor mis-

takes, he would lose time coming out of the turn. He would also lose races.

Amidst the roar of cars hot-lapping, Doug heard one particular engine winding up as its driver raced down the straightaway and into the turn. But there was no hesitation as he released the throttle and hit the brakes. The engine kept revving long past the point when Doug's senses told him the driver should have lifted his foot. Instead, there was a dull thud—the sound of a race car slamming into the wall, a sound that mechanics, accustomed as they are to noise, do not like to hear. Doug knew from the severeness of the impact that the driver of that race car was hurt. He turned around and realized it was Danny.

Jimmy Caruthers, meanwhile, continued hot-lapping. When he came down the straightaway and into the first turn, he saw his brother's car sitting against the outside wall. There was no damage to the car on the left side; it appeared as though Danny merely parked it against the wall. Jimmy slid on past, powering out into the back straightaway, wondering what happened. Maybe Danny's engine quit, Jimmy thought. As he replayed the scene in his mind, he suddenly realized Danny was leaning forward in his seat.

A cold sweat broke out on the back of Jimmy's neck.

On the back turn a corner worker signaled Jimmy to slow down. He braked for the turn, as usual, but made no attempt to stomp on the throttle coming out of it. People in the grandstand were standing, looking toward turn one. They seemed strangely silent. The starter waved his yellow flag.

People from the pits ran onto the track to gather around Danny's car. Doug was among them. Flames rose beneath the car, a spark from the engine having ignited spilled oil. But even as Jimmy, approaching slowly, began to worry about the threat of fire, someone appeared with a fire extinguisher. The car vanished momentarily behind a cloud of white dust. The flames died.

Jimmy halted his car at the end of the straightaway, yanked the gear shift lever into a neutral position, and jumped out without bothering to cut his engine. Gary Bettenhausen pulled in behind him and also ran to help.

Jimmy reached his brother's side and pushed several people away. He saw Danny was unconscious. He also saw a trickle of blood on his face, coming from beneath his helmet. Doug was standing there beside him. "Goddam it!" said Doug.

"What the hell happened?" Jimmy asked.

"Goddam it! I told Danny to fasten those shoulder harnesses. When he hit the wall, he bumped his head on the roll cage."

Jimmy unbuckled his brother's chin strap and slowly raised the helmet from his head. The blood came from a wound on Danny's forehead. A discolored knot already began to rise. Danny's crash helmet had not protected him from the sudden blow.

"How did he crash?"

"His throttle stuck."

"Shit," said Jimmy Caruthers.

He reached down and unfastened his brother's lap belt. His hands trembled as he did so. Jimmy could visualize what happened. In the last instant before Danny lost control, he stabbed at the kill button, which would have cut his engine. But it was in the wrong place.

"Shit," said Jimmy Caruthers.

An ambulance pulled onto the track behind him. Jimmy looked up and saw the attendants climbing out of the ambulance and coming toward him. "Handle him carefully," Jimmy instructed them. He helped lift his brother out of the race car and placed him in the ambulance. Doug climbed into the ambulance's front seat and the ambulance headed out the track gate to the hospital, its red light flashing. Jimmy turned around and saw his race car had been moved by someone back to the pits.

He walked in that direction. People seemed to move out of his way. Nobody said much. Someone finally asked, "Hey, how is he?"

"He's junk!"

The person seemed startled by the bluntness of the remark. Jimmy's eyes betrayed no emotion. He sat down on the tailgate of his pickup truck. Junk. Danny Caruthers, USAC midget champion, was now junk.

A wrecker towed Danny's damaged race car from the track. The people in the stands were sitting down now. The mechanics returned to their cars and began to line them up on the main straightaway ready for the continuation of the program. The feature event would be run with or without Danny Caruthers.

Before Doug Caruthers left for the hospital, his brother, Red, asked him, "What do you want done with the cars?"

"Park them or race them," said Doug. "I don't care."

Afterwards Red went to look for his nephew. He found Jimmy sitting in his race car at the starting line, waiting for the feature event to begin. "Are you okay?" he asked him.

"I'm okay."

"Are you sure you want to race?"

"I'm sure."

The starter waved the green flag. Racing continued. The feature event was seventy-five laps on the half-mile track. Jimmy failed to finish. His quick-change gear burned out midway through the race while he was running in third place. The track crew pushed him out of the way onto an escape road near turn four. Jimmy sat next to his car, waiting for the feature to end so he could go to the hospital. One of the track workers asked about Danny. Jimmy merely shook his head.

"Is he that bad?"

"He's got a knot on his head this big." Jimmy held up his hand to demonstrate.

There was a long silence, punctuated only by the scream of midget engines.

"I had to get back in that car," Jimmy said finally. "If I didn't, I don't know if I could ever get into a race car again."

Afterwards, Jimmy went to the hospital in Riverside. Danny was still clinging to life, and he continued to cling for five more days. Each of those days his mother visited him. Jimmy accompanied her, much to his discomfort. He could see no reason for hanging around the hospital. He already had written his brother off. On the fifth day Danny died, and Jimmy was relieved because he knew he could get on with the rest of his life.

One of the ambulance drivers later claimed that if the crowd waited until they arrived before moving Danny, he might have survived. There were a lot of if's surrounding Danny's death, but Jimmy was buying none of them.

"Shit," he said.

Later Doug asked his only remaining son, "Do you want to give up racing?"

Jimmy Caruthers shook his head. "I can't quit now. It's what I want to do."

5

After Danny died a lot of people got angry with Jimmy Caruthers because he sat at the speaker's table at the USAC awards banquet, joking with Gary Bettenhausen. Doug was accepting the award for Danny's posthumous championship, and Jimmy paid no attention.

The speech lasted nearly ten minutes and made Jimmy nervous. It reminded him that someday he might end the way his brother ended—bent over a wheel, unconscious, at the end of some straightaway, up against the wall after having lost control.

Danny's death affected Jimmy much more than most people realized. Night after night afterwards he couldn't sleep. He walked the floor at home. He could not close his eyes after helping to lift Danny out of that race car. He tried to close them, then remembered running up to the side of his kid brother's midget, taking Danny's helmet off, seeing all that blood.

So he joked to hide his sorrow—and fear. Like the remark he made to car builder Don Edmunds about the deal money, which in USAC midget racing goes each race the following season to the defending champion, the driver with number one on his car. If the champion fails to show, the number two driver gets the deal money. It hardly amounted to much—maybe $50 or $75 a race.

Jimmy wanted an opportunity to get back at Edmunds ever since the latter's buddy, a drag racer, killed himself at a drag race near Irvine. The guy crashed badly, decapitating himself, and made the front pages of all the California newspapers. Jimmy appeared at Edmunds' shop the next morning to offer condolences: "I'm sorry to hear about your buddy."

"Yeah," said Edmunds. "I hear he lost his head at the drags."

So after Danny died and Edmunds offered condolences, Jimmy replied, "Well, at least I'll get his deal money next year."

Jimmy wasn't interested in Danny's deal money. He had helped his brother win the championship by giving him both advice and, on several occasions, his own race car.

Race drivers often joke about death. It is one of their methods for coping with it. Most race drivers are jokers anyway. Among professional athletes they are the most kinetic outside the arena. Few other athletes display such traces of madness, have such a penchant for mischief, or cause such destruction (particularly to rental cars).

Basketball players display a style that might be described as medium cool. They smile infrequently. They eye strangers suspiciously. Their travel schedules often include five games in five cities in five nights, a pace so hectic they barely have time to eat, sleep, and perform before catching the next plane.

Football players act more like executives. They are corporation men, more likely to be seen carrying an attaché case than a gym bag. They practice only a few hours a day, play only a few games a season, and spend their time worrying about the stock market.

Baseball players (particularly bullpen pitchers) come closest to auto racers in their penchant for devilment. They are big men playing a little boy's game. The pace of that game is sufficiently slow to provide them time to devise tricks to play on teammates.

But *nobody* has more time on their hands than race drivers, particularly those who drive championship cars. They spend long hours in towns where nothing happens unless they make it happen. A racer may drive two practice laps around a track like Indy, pull into the pits, then wait four hours for his crew to make an adjustment to permit him to drive two *more* laps. To become a successful auto racer you must not only possess instant reflexes, but you also need a high tolerance for boredom. A driver has nothing else to do many days but lounge around the pits, smoke too many cigarettes, and think about the dangers of his profession. Auto racers, like bullfighters, face death every time they step into the arena, a fact of which they are painfully aware, whether they admit it or not.

Yet death did not frighten Jimmy Caruthers. What frightened Jimmy was the possibility of losing control—the threat that someday he might not be able to live fast and do all the things he wanted to do, which only partially included going two hundred miles per hour at Indianapolis.

Jimmy Caruthers slid sideways, dragging his left foot along the concrete just the way he saw Burritto do it at the motorcycle races. For a moment it seemed as though the cycle would slide out from under him, but he jerked the handlebars, pipped the throttle, and regained his balance, shouting and screaming at the top of his lungs.

Jerry McClung came careening up behind him. "Hey, Caruthers! One side or a leg off!" McClung shot by outside

Caruthers, cut him off, skidded in a tight circle, narrowly missing a heavy wooden beam planted at the edge of the concrete. He revved his motorcycle full throttle, doing a wheelie.

"Hey, you hot dog. You cut me off!"

"Tough luck, Caruthers!"

They slid around another turn, their cycles jumping, jerking, screeching. Jimmy moved up beside his friend and tried to execute the same maneuver by which he had just been passed.

But going around the next turn he leaned too much inside, losing his balance. The bike slid out from under him and crashed into the heavy wooden beam. *Keerakk!* Jimmy tumbled head first into his own motorcycle. *Whoomp!*

Jimmy got up limping, rubbing his leg. It felt sore from where he slid across the concrete, but it did not seem broken. His motorcycle, laying on its side, wounded but not dying, somehow still was running. He yanked the bike upright and jumped on again. He popped it back in gear and charged after Jerry McClung.

He and Jerry were riding that morning in the desert around Phoenix, out past the end of Base Line Road, when they found the old barn. The barn was like a relic abandoned in the desert. It was coming apart. All that remained was a roof, pillars, and concrete floor. "Looks like a hell of a spot for a motorcycle race," suggested Caruthers.

"Why the hell not?" agreed Jerry McClung.

So they cycled up a ramp onto the concrete floor and started racing each other, skidding and sliding and falling down and banging into the wooden posts and otherwise having the time of their lives.

Jimmy, back on his bike, went roaring after his friend now, cutting the corners short to catch him. He moved outside to pass, but saw he could not get by. The two bumped. A wooden post loomed ahead. "Oh shit!" Jimmy jerked his handlebars right and sailed out of the barn, off the concrete floor (which was raised several feet above the ground), out into space, soaring like Evel Knievel. "Hellllpp!" He landed with a bounce, almost fell off, caught his balance for a moment, then went down in a pile again. Jimmy lay in a heap, then rolled over on his back. He was motionless.

Jerry McClung, still circling inside the gutted barn, looked over his shoulder and saw his friend lying there. For one moment a hint of worry crossed his mind, but hell, you never knew what Jimmy Caruthers might pull. He halted his cycle and waited for Jimmy to say something. He finally shouted, "Hey, good buddy. You all right?"

"Hahahahahahaha."

Jerry gunned his engine and headed straight to the edge of the concrete floor, sailed out into space, but landed smoothly, with hardly a quiver. He braked his machine at the point where Jimmy still lay laughing on the ground. "You got more bravery than brains, Caruthers," McClung shouted over his idling engine. "You better stick to four wheels and stay away from two."

"This is great," sighed Jimmy. "We ought to charge admission."

"Yeah," Jerry agreed. "If we don't kill each other first."

McClung cut his engine, got off, and sat down near Jimmy Caruthers on the ground. Jimmy rolled over on his back, cradling his head with his palms, and stared up at the cloudless sky. For a moment neither man talked; the only sound was their heavy breathing. Finally Jimmy broke the silence: "So you're not going back." He meant the statement as a question.

"Nope," answered his friend.

"There's going to be some good times back there this summer."

No reply.

Jimmy began to think of all the reasons why a driver as

talented as Jerry McClung might decide against making racing his career. He knew the reasons well, having considered them in his own case with opposite results. Jerry had gone with Jimmy twice to the Midwest and in two years of hard work had placed fourth in the USAC standings twice. That was good, but not good enough to have the champ car owners beating on his garage door. Jimmy placed first and second in the standings and they were hardly beating on his either.

"There's going to be some bad times back there, too," Jerry finally said.

"Yeah, there is," Jimmy agreed.

They fell silent again, the desert still around them. Jimmy thought about the long hours each night working on the cars, the exhausting travel from track to track, the little money to be won, the dangers at the end of each straightaway. That was the bad of it, but that was the good of it, too. Sooner or later, however, there came a time when you either had to get up or get out. Get up in a better division with more money and less work, or leave the circuit and go back to the other part of your life, your wife, your family, while there was still wife and family to go back to.

He knew his friend decided to get out not from fear, but from lack of desire. Jerry liked the desert, liked working on dune buggies in his garage, liked stopping off for a beer with the boys after work, liked being around his family and sleeping in the same bed with the same woman each night. He probably would race weekends at nearby Manzanita, become a local hero again, and have fun doing it. That was all right for Jerry McClung, but not for Jimmy Caruthers.

Would the decisions have been the same if he had been the one finishing fourth two years while Jerry McClung, or Dave Strickland, won championships? Strickland was off the circuit, too, now, running a liquor store in Denver.

Jimmy sighed. Jerry McClung was a good friend, but he

was about to drop out of Jimmy's life. If things had been different, would Jimmy be back on the Coast working in the mobile home business instead of heading off to Indianapolis, bound on fulfillment of what might become an impossible dream? If not this year, would he be back there next year, or the year after, or twenty years from now? Jimmy Caruthers did not know, and he planned to waste no more time worrying about it.

"Let's get on with it!" Jimmy Caruthers shouted and sprang to his feet.

"What's the next race on the program?" asked McClung.

"Trophy dash. Four laps around the barn."

"And whoever loses buys the beer."

When Jimmy returned to the Midwest for the start of the summer racing season, he continued to date Suzie Grim, but not openly. He wanted as few people to know it as possible. Jimmy still remained legally tied to his wife back in California, despite that relationship's being, for all practical purposes, over. Jimmy and Sally were not yet divorced and he did not want to do anything that would embarrass her, or their son, young Jimmy. He also did not want to embarrass Suzie. "We shouldn't be seen in public," Jimmy cautioned her, so when they dated, they went out alone, and to places away from the west side of Indianapolis.

Suzie, however, did not seem embarrassed by their relationship. She felt no shame because, by their second date, she had fallen completely in love with Jimmy Caruthers. Until that moment Suzie had never cared for anybody before, not deeply, and it was a unique experience. It just seemed natural for her and Jimmy to be together. She wondered why, after knowing him as a friend for so many years, it had taken her so long to discover her love for him.

Jimmy liked Suzie because Suzie liked racing. It was as much a part of her background as his. He was comfortable with her. He could talk about what interested him without worrying about whether it interested her. He could drive to a race with her and go about his business without worrying about whether she was bored or not. She had as many friends at the track as he. In fact, they were the same friends.

Suzie realized that Jimmy's goals had become her goals. She prayed for his success in racing. She wanted him to get a championship car ride and drive at Indy, maybe even someday win the 500. She wanted to participate in his glory. After her moment of panic a year before, when she almost married someone she did not love, she no longer worried about being an old maid. Being with Jimmy was enough, sharing with him the thrill of racing. It was now the right thing for her to do, and she would let the future take care of itself. As for Jimmy, he was too wrapped up in his own goals to realize they had become Suzie's goals as well.

In April Jimmy drove in the Tony Hulman Classic, a sprint car race in Terre Haute, Indiana. Sprint cars look like midgets, but have more powerful engines and are more dangerous. During the race he bumped another car. The impact of the collision sent him flipping end over end. "Before he finished flipping," Suzie confessed later, "I was in the ambulance."

Jimmy was unconscious when they lifted him out of the race car, but recovered before reaching the hospital. He had no serious injuries, but did very little sprint car racing after that. He did not like that breed of race car. Jimmy did not want to get hurt in one and endanger his chances to race at Indy.

After Suzie returned from the hospital, Dana Ward (who was then dating Jimmy's father) told her, "Well, if anybody doesn't know you and Jim are going together, they know now."

After Jimmy's divorce became final, he moved into Suzie

Grim's apartment. Theirs became a marriage of convenience rather than a marriage by decree. They kept their living arrangement secret at first from Suzie's parents. Suzie's mother eventually found out, but neglected to relay that information to Bobby Grim. Suzie's father continued to believe Jimmy roomed with another driver and merely dated his daughter.

Jimmy did not wish to remarry. He never hid his feelings on this subject. Suzie knew what was in his mind. Jimmy's mother and father were divorced, his father divorced once before that, and he had been caught in the middle. He remembered their constant arguing. Now he was divorced and had a son caught in the middle. At least he could spare his son any arguing. He seemed wary to repeat his mistake. It was difficult for a race driver to stay married, and he knew it. Although he loved Suzie and, in one sense, left his wife for her, he did not want to marry her. "I'm not ready yet," he apologized to her.

"I understand," Suzie replied.

She knew Jimmy wanted to be free to live his own life, to come and go as he wanted without being hemmed in again. Suzie may not have liked this arrangement, even though she told herself and others she did, but she accepted the arrangement and appeared happy with it. Perhaps she loved Jimmy so much, and shared his goals in auto racing so much that she was willing to accept whatever portion of him he willingly gave her.

In May Jimmy Caruthers appeared at the Indianapolis Motor Speedway as Clint Brawner's driver. Compared to the major teams, Brawner came to the Speedway underfinanced and with the same Scorpion car that proved barely competitive the previous season. Jimmy had on the side of his car, "the US Armed Services," his main sponsor, as well as Steed, an oil product, but they did not provide as much money as did, say STP's Andy Granatelli, for whom Art Pollard was back running in 1972.

Pollard qualified easily, then slammed his car into the wall while practicing and broke his leg. Jimmy went to visit him in the hospital and pasted an STP decal on Art's forehead. Art, lying in bed with a cast on his leg, was frustrated at missing the 500. He explained that a hub failed, causing the accident: "When something breaks, there's nowhere to go but into the wall."

Jimmy qualified, but precariously, with a slow time. He worried that other faster cars might bump him from the race. Although on the surface the qualifying system at Indianapolis seems complex, with drivers qualifying in different positions on different days, basically it boiled down to: the thirty-three fastest drivers made the race. On Saturday evening of the final weekend of qualifications, he retained his precarious position. If two more drivers posted faster times, he would watch the 500 from the grandstand again, a prospect he found uninviting.

The qualification trials continued Sunday afternoon. As the six o'clock closing time approached, Jimmy paced anxiously in the pits. Suzie waited in the Tower Terrace grandstand nearby. She had in her purse a wrapped gift, a stainless steel cigarette lighter she planned to offer as a consolation prize in case he failed to make the field. With the tension increasing, she decided not to wait and ran down to the fence separating spectators from racers. She called to Jimmy. He walked to the fence looking glum, frightened. "What's up, Babe?"

"I was going to give you this later," Suzie explained. "I think you need it now." She handed him the package.

Jimmy tore off the wrapping paper and discovered the lighter. It had on its side a drawing of the "Peanuts" cartoon character, Snoopy, driving a race car. Underneath was the motto "Aaah! The Hell With It!"

Jimmy smiled for the first time that afternoon. "Boy, I'll go along with that. That's exactly how I feel." He kissed Suzie, pressed her hand, and stuffed the lighter in his uniform pocket and returned his attention to the remaining cars attempting to qualify, feeling temporarily relieved.

At 6:00 PM, a pistol poked out the window of the tower near the starting line. It went off with a bang. The end of qualifications and Jimmy Caruthers remained thirty-second fastest. Lee Kunzman, another rookie, stood thirty-first, a narrow margin separating both drivers from anonymity.

Kunzman and Caruthers had gotten to know each other while driving the midget circuit. Lee Kunzman came from Guttenberg, Iowa, a conservative farm town in the middle of the corn belt. He claimed Jimmy showed him how to wear Levis, taught him how to relax. That night Jimmy and Lee celebrated their success with Suzie and Lee's girl friend, Bev Kirby, a stewardess for United Airlines. The two young drivers managed to get magnificently drunk. The following weekend, on the morning of the race Jimmy rode to the track with Suzie on the back of his motorcycle. She worried because she knew the dangers of driving at Indianapolis, particularly the breathtaking moment when the green flag drops, signaling the start of the race, and all thirty-three drivers rush for position going into the first turn. She worried that after she kissed him good-bye the morning of the race, she might never see him alive again. She wanted him in the race and yet she did not want him in the race. Suzie tried not to let Jimmy know how upset she was, but failed. As he started to walk into Gasoline Alley, tears appeared in her eyes.

Jimmy began to smile. "What's the matter with your eyes?"

"Oh nothing," said Suzie bravely.

"What do you mean, nothing? Are those tears?"

"No."

Jimmy glared at her in mock anger. "Those are tears! I thought you were supposed to be brave. Haven't you been around racing long enough to know that it makes great warriors nervous when their silly girl friends cry as they go into battle?"

"I'm not crying," said Suzie, crying.

"You're not?"

"I think I have something in my eyes," she stammered.

"It's a sty."

"Sty, my eye."

"No, my eye!"

"Your eye?"

"Oh, go race!" Now she was laughing instead of crying. She dabbed at her eyes with a handkerchief.

He stared at her for several seconds. "I shall return carrying my shield or being carried upon it."

"Where did you learn that one?"

"Fullerton Junior College. I shall return with my sword held high."

"Your sword's always high. That's one of your problems, Caruthers."

"I shall return with the laurel wreath of victory on my brow."

"Shut up, Caruthers, and go race." She kissed him and pushed him toward his garage.

It was the year of the rookie at Indianapolis. Eight new drivers qualified for the 500 in 1972, more than double the usual number. In addition to Kunzman and Caruthers, there was Sam Posey, Mike Hiss, John Martin, John Mahler, Swede Savage, and Salt Walther.

Everyone's favorite for rookie of the year honors was Savage, a protégé of retired Grand Prix driver Dan Gurney. Swede Savage already had placed high in several championship car races. Like Jimmy, Swede grew up in California driving quarter midgets. Swede Savage resembled Danny Caruthers in that he was a flashy, exciting, fearless driver, one who seemed determined to succeed. He suffered a concussion after crashing badly in a Formula A car at Ontario, California, in the fall of 1971, but recovered and climbed back into the cockpit again. He qualified ninth at Indy.

But even the most promising drivers are at the mercy of their equipment. A broken connecting rod ended Swede Savage's chances early. One by one the other rookies dropped from the race. Only three remained on the track when the checkered flag fell. Sam Posey, seventh qualifier, placed fifth. Mike Hiss, who started twenty-fifth, moved up to seventh. Jimmy Caruthers took ninth. The rookie of the year award went to Hiss. Suzie was angry, feeling Jimmy should have received the award.

Nothing made Jimmy angry, however—not even the fact that Lee Kunzman almost put him into the wall midway through the race. Lee's right rear tire was going flat without him realizing it. As Jimmy lapped him in turn three, the flattening tire caused Lee to skid slightly sideways. His right rear touched Jimmy's left front tire.

"Hey, you damn near made me crash out there," Jimmy chided his friend afterwards, "and there wasn't anything I could do about it because I couldn't take you into the wall with me."

At Michigan International Speedway in July a burned piston blew out the bottom of the engine in Jimmy's Scorpion, spraying the track with oil and causing the race to be halted for nearly an hour. After the restart, Gary Bettenhausen's brother, Merle, driving in his first championship race, slid coming out of the second turn and catapulted into the guardrail. His arm flew out of the cockpit and the rail severed it from his body. The race again was halted for nearly an hour as workers cleared the track.

During the interim period Jimmy climbed into George Snider's car. Snider fell from his motorcycle several days before, injuring his shoulder and causing him problems in the high-banked turns. Jimmy, driving Snider's car, finished fourth, his best finish to that date.

"Right now I'm to the point where I'm established as a championship driver," he later told an interviewing reporter. "If something happens to the Brawner deal, I could step into another car without too much trouble, perhaps even into a better car. That's a hard rung to get to—establishing yourself as someone a car owner will trust to jump into his race car on a minute's notice, trusting you not to do something foolish that might tear up his equipment."

While the owners now knew Jimmy Caruthers, the track guards did not. Two weeks later Jimmy drove in the Pocono 500. One day during practice, while Brawner labored on his race car, Jimmy accompanied Lee Kunzman to the pits. Lee wore his driver's uniform and walked behind his race car. Jimmy wore his standard relaxing uniform—levis and a T-shirt. He looked more like someone who drank beer and threw frisbees in the infield rather than one of the drivers. He pedaled a bicycle alongside Kunzman, conversing with him.

After Kunzman climbed into his car, Jimmy decided to return to the garage area. A track guard blocked his path: "You can't come in here."

"But I'm one of the drivers. I'm Jimmy Caruthers."

"Let's see your identification badge."

Jimmy fumbled in his pockets, but came up with nothing. "I must have left the badge in my truck."

"Then you'll have to go to your truck and get it. You can't come through here without an identification badge."

"Look, can't you let me ride through here and go to my truck for my badge, and I'll come back and show it to you?"

The guard shook his head. Rules were rules.

Jimmy shrugged. A believer in law and order, he returned to the pits, looking for an exit to the parking lot where he left his pickup truck. He pedaled from one end of the pits to the other, but found no exit except through the garage area. He could be trapped in the pits the rest of his life, for all that guard cared.

Finally, Jimmy began pedaling his bike at top speed. He whisked past the guard and through the gate into the garage area.

"Come back here!" shouted the guard, running after Jimmy. Jimmy wheeled around the corner on his bike and zipped into the garage, where Brawner was working on his race car. Clint glanced up, surprised. The guard approached at a run, now accompanied by two other guards.

Jimmy grabbed Clint by the arm and propelled his mechanic into the guards' path. "Tell them who I am!"

Later, everybody at Pocono learned who Jimmy Caruthers was. Midway through the race he ran over some debris and flattened his left front tire. The blowout occurred on the straightaway, so he kept the car under control and pulled into the pits for new rubber. He returned to the track, and within a few laps punctured his right rear tire.

Unfortunately the tire blew in a turn with most of the car's weight on that outside tire. Jimmy's race car skidded out of control and up into the outside wall. The shattering crash ruptured the fuel tanks.

Suzie stood on the top row of the grandstand. She watched Jimmy's car explode in flames on impact. For a moment panic gripped her. Would she be widowed without ever having been married? Then the track announcer broadcast, "Caruthers is out of the race car. And it looks like he's all right." Suzie started to relax.

A few minutes later one of Jimmy's crewmen rushed into the stands. "Let's go," he said.

"What's wrong?"

"Just come with me."

"Is he hurt?" asked Suzie, but the crewman dragged her down the stairs, through the garage area gates, out to the field hospital. As they arrived, the ambulance drove up with Jimmy in the back. White foam from the fire extinguishers blanketed his uniform. An oxygen mask hid his face. He did not seem to be moving. Suzie's first reaction was that *he's dead!*

But when the nurse removed the oxygen mask, Suzie realized he was not. "My leg hurts!" Jimmy screamed. The nurse immediately stuck a needle in him. It was a shot of morphine to relieve the pain. He lapsed into a state of semiconsciousness.

For the second time Suzie climbed into the back of an ambulance. It sped away from the field hospital, out of the racetrack, light flashing, siren screaming, and headed for the highway and Stroudsburg Hospital, thirty miles distant. The morphine shot made Jimmy drowsy. He slept, then woke, then slept again. One time when he opened his eyes he saw Suzie leaning over him, smiling.

"It's not funny," he said.

"I know," she replied.

At Stroudsburg Hospital a doctor examined Jimmy briefly in the emergency room. "He seems merely to have burned himself on his hands and ankles," the doctor explained to Suzie. She rasied her hand to her mouth, anxious about the burns, but relieved his injuries were not worse. The burns on his hands occurred when he braced himself on the edge of the cockpit to lift himself out of the car. The cockpit edge was so hot that it burned through his safety gloves.

"How soon can you get me out of here?" asked Jimmy, glancing nervously around at the sterile-looking emergency room with its white walls and stacks of pharmaceutical supplies and medical equipment in corners and on tables. The hospital atmosphere made him nervous. It reminded him of his mortality.

"Well, the burns don't seem serious enough to keep you in the hospital," suggested the doctor. "As soon as we have a chance to examine the X-rays, just to make sure nothing is broken, we'll sign you out."

Jimmy turned to Suzie: "See if you can call Pop. If he hears the news on the radio, he's going to be worried."

Suzie located a pay telephone and fumbled in her purse for some change. Doug was at a midget race in Springfield, Illinois, that weekend. She dreaded making the call, knowing they would page Doug at the track. Having had one son killed in racing, he immediately would suspect the worst. It would worry him. But Jimmy was right. He would worry more if he learned only half of the news.

It seemed like an eternity before Doug came to the phone. "Hello!" he shouted. She could hear the roar of engines in the background.

"Doug, it's Suzie."

"What?"

Doug was somewhat hard of hearing. She shouted into the phone, "Doug, Jimmy had an accident, but he's all right now."

"What the hell happened?"

"He punctured a tire and hit the wall. He has some burns, nothing serious."

"That fool kid."

"We'll be leaving the hospital as soon as the doctors finish looking at the X-rays."

"You scared me," were Doug's last words before hanging up.

Suzie returned to the emergency room and found Jimmy looking downcast, his shoulders slumped forward as though carrying the weight of the world on his back. "Doug said—" she began, then halted. "What's wrong?"

"Well, Babe," Jimmy sighed. "I guess we're not going home tonight."

"Why not?"

"The doctor says I have a broken leg."

It was a traumatic experience for Suzie Grim and Jimmy

Caruthers. The leg did not break when he hit the wall, but apparently when he wrenched it loose from the crumpled body metal to escape the flames. People later kept telling him how lucky he was, not to have been more seriously injured, and Suzie would agree, but a broken leg meant the season was over. It meant quitting racing at a time when he seemed on the verge of stardom. Once out of a car for six months, or whatever time it took the leg to heal, he would lose his touch—or so Jimmy feared. He could even lose his ride. Brawner might hire another driver. Other owners would not understand the crash was not his fault. Reputations fade fast in racing.

The newspapers carried photographs of Jimmy's crash the next morning—multiple exposures showing each bump, each grind. Jimmy seemed fascinated with the photos, particularly one photo that showed a massive track worker cradling him in his arms, lifting him from the wrecked race car, ready to place him in the ambulance. Jimmy slowly shook his head. "I don't even remember that happening."

The doctors released him from the hospital that morning, his leg set and placed in a cast. Car owner Gene White of Atlanta volunteered to fly Suzie and Jimmy back to Indianapolis by private plane.

Suzie's father waited at the Indianapolis airport to drive Jimmy to Methodist Hospital for another medical examination. The doctors at Methodist X-rayed the leg through the cast, decided there was no reason to retain him in the hospital, and said he could go home. Doug Caruthers arrived and suggested Jimmy stay in his house. Suzie's mother suggested that Jimmy stay with the Grims.

Jimmy settled the argument: "Listen, if I go anywhere, it will be to our apartment!"

At the mention of "our" apartment, Bobby Grim turned and looked at his daughter. Then he looked at his wife. She shrugged. It was his first realization that Jimmy and

Suzie were living together. Nevertheless, Suzie's father helped take Jimmy to their apartment, even helping to carry him upstairs and put him in bed.

Suzie thought her dad was very cool. He never said a word.

That week a reporter stopped by the apartment to interview Jimmy for a book on auto racing. Jimmy sat in a wheelchair, dressed in a pair of cut-off jeans, wearing a white T-shirt bearing the red insignia of "Ashland," a gasoline company that helped sponsor his race car. His leg was in a cast, his hands wrapped in bandages. "What about the element of risk?" the reporter asked.

"The older you get, the more it bothers you." Jimmy admitted. "When I was twenty-one, I didn't think about it. Now, once in a while I do start getting flashes about things that happen—not while I'm driving, but sometimes while I'm sleeping. It doesn't bother you until the last instant. It's that instant before you hit that keeps flashing back, the moment when you sit back there, thinking 'Oh, this is going to hurt.'"

"Then what?" prodded the reporter.

Jimmy looked at him for a second, recognizing that the reporter was probing for man's reaction to his own impending death. He thought, why is the press always hung up on death and dying? He did not know whether he wanted to share his thoughts on that subject with others. Finally, he smiled. "It's three-two-one, Conkle."

"Three-two-one, Conkle?" The reporter seemed puzzled.

"Those are the braking numbers on the wall as you come down the straightaway at Indianapolis," Jimmy explained. "First you pass the three. Then the two. Then the one. Then it's Conkle."

"Conkle?"

"The funeral home on sixteenth street, two blocks down

from the Speedway. If you haven't hit your brakes by the time you pass one, they call Conkle."

After the reporter left, Jimmy shouted to Suzie, "My leg is killing me!"

Suzie went to work each morning, leaving Jimmy alone in the apartment with nothing to do but watch soap operas and game shows on television. "What do you women see in these things anyhow?" he asked.

Suzie arrived home each night and tried to boost his spirits by kidding him: "How come you didn't take the garbage downstairs?"

"Gee, I forgot."

After several days of isolation, Jimmy could stand the boredom no longer. One day when Suzie left for work he crawled down the stairway from their second-floor apartment to his pickup truck in the parking lot. He carried with him a long-handled device that Clint Brawner once used, when he had a broken leg, to operate the brake pedal. Jimmy headed over to the Speedway and spent the day hanging around Gasoline Alley. One of his friends later drove back with him to the apartment and carried him upstairs. When Suzie arrived home from work that evening, Jimmy looked up from his wheelchair and said, "God, it's boring doing nothing all day."

Gene Romero arrived in town. During the summer Burritto usually operated out of Indianapolis, often staying with Jimmy and Suzie overnight. Jimmy arranged for him to garage his motorcycles at Dave Laycock's shop in nearby Danbury. Laycock had a motorcycle distributorship next to his home and a lot of fields out back for riding, as well as a small pond for fishing.

Burritto told Suzie he would take Jimmy to the hospital for his checkup one week after the accident. "Can I trust you?" she said.

"Suzie, you know me," said Burritto.

"That's what I mean."

Burritto arrived at the apartment after Suzie left for work and cradled Jimmy in his arms to carry him downstairs to the pickup truck. Jimmy began to complain, "Drop me and I'll sue."

"If I drop you, Caruthers, there won't be enough left of you to sue." Burritto made a motion to pitch his friend over the rail.

"Hey!"

"What's wrong, Caruthers? Are you afraid to die?"

"If it's falling off a second-floor balcony, yes."

They drove to the hospital. Burritto obtained a wheelchair and pushed Jimmy down a long corridor toward the doctor's office. The doctor examined Jimmy's cast, informed him the leg seemed to be coming along, and asked him to return for another examination the following Thursday. "That was quick," remarked Burritto.

"Yeah, a quick buck for the doctor."

"You better get a second job to pay for the bills."

"I've got accident insurance."

Burritto pushed open the door at the end of the corridor. They were atop a long ramp leading to the sidewalk. "Adios, amigo," said Burritto, and gave Jimmy a push.

"Romero, you're trying to kill me!" shouted Jimmy, his chair picking up speed rolling down the ramp.

"Don't worry. You've got accident insurance."

Afterwards they stopped by the Speedway, drove out to Laycock's shop, then came back to the apartment and sat around talking. Burritto left just before Suzie arrived home from work at 5:30. "Well, what happened today?" she asked.

"Nothing much," said Jimmy.

His leg continued to bother him, particularly his ankle, which hurt continuously. The cast covered the ankle as well as the leg, and Jimmy wondered if the ankle might be burned, something the doctors in Stroudsburg overlooked. "Maybe I ought to have the cast taken off so they can look at it," Jimmy worried.

He called his doctor, but only succeeded in talking to one of the receptionists. "Since you have an appointment for next Thursday, why not wait until then?"

Jimmy slammed the telephone down. He was angry, frustrated. "You never get any answers out of these doctors," he snapped.

"What do you want to do?" asked Suzie.

"I don't know."

Jimmy asked Suzie to bring him a can of beer from the refrigerator. He sat in his wheelchair, sipping the beer slowly, thinking. The inactivity was beginning to grind on him. It got on his nerves; then he got on Suzie's nerves, which he did not want to do. What bothered him was that he was unconvinced that the medical people in charge of his case were doing as much as they could to help him get back in a car as soon as possible. That was his number one goal.

Then he remembered Mike Hiss. Mike broke his leg while riding a motorcycle shortly after the Indy 500. It did not take him six months to return to racing. Mike found a doctor near his home in California who placed a pin in his leg and fitted a special boot on him. He did not miss a single race, although at first he had difficulty convincing USAC officials he was fit to drive a race car.

Jimmy found Mike at home in Tustin, California, a small community just south of Anaheim. "What's happening, Jimmy?" asked the other driver.

"Hey, Mike, what's the name of that doctor who said the mumbo jumbo over your leg and made it well again?"

"His name is Dr. Callaghan. He's got an office here in Tustin."

Jimmy hung up the telephone and told Suzie, "I'm going to California."

His mother met him at the Los Angeles airport. The next day Jimmy Caruthers sat in the examining room of Michael F. Callaghan, M.D., a large man with a cheery disposition. "No wonder your ankle has been bothering you," said Dr. Callaghan.

"Why, what's wrong?"

"It's broken, too."

Jimmy closed his eyes and slowly shook his head. "Oh, that's beautiful," he groaned. "Just beautiful." He did not know whether to laugh or cry. He could not understand how the physicians in both Stroudsberg and Indianapolis failed to detect the broken ankle in addition to the broken leg.

"These things sometimes happen," explained Dr. Callaghan.

"I understand that," said Jimmy, "But why to me?"

Dr. Callaghan told his patient not to worry, that he could repair the damage and place pins in his leg as he did with Mike Hiss. One question was paramount in Jimmy Caruthers' mind: "How soon can I race?"

"When's your next event?"

"The Ontario 500 over Labor Day weekend."

"You'll be ready," promised Dr. Callaghan. A wide smile spread over Jimmy Caruthers' face.

After Jimmy returned to his mother's home, he called Suzie to tell her the news. She was happy to hear he would be racing again, but furious at what happened: "Aren't you angry at those other doctors for what they did?"

"There's no sense getting angry," he tried to calm her. "That's ancient history."

"But your leg might have been permanently damaged." Her voice was cold, angry. Suzie Grim remembered all the other race drivers she knew with twisted arms, mangled hands, burns, scars, and those who always walked with a limp. Suzie did not want Jimmy changed from the way she knew him.

"It didn't happen," he insisted in a firm voice. "Dr. Callaghan said I would be better than ever."

"He's just saying that so you won't sue those other doctors."

"Don't worry, Babe. I trust him. He's a good doctor, one of the best I've met."

"Well, if you trust him, I trust him." Suzie said it, but she didn't mean it.

Jimmy checked into the hospital in early August for the operation to repair his leg and ankle. Tustin Community Hospital was a sprawling, one-story medical facility a few blocks south of the San Diego Freeway and only about a ten-minute drive from Jimmy's mother's house in Anaheim. Many hospitals appear sterile and foreboding and almost reek of sickness and death; not Tustin Community. It was designed like a Spanish hacienda with adobe walls, tile roof, a slate floor in the waiting room, carpets in the corridors, bright paintings on the corridor walls. The hospital frequently treated race drivers, partly because of its location near Orange County Drag Strip. In addition to Jimmy Caruthers and Mike Hiss, drag racer Gene Snow and land record holder Gary Gabelich recovered from racing injuries at Tustin Community Hospital.

Nevertheless, Jimmy Caruthers acquired the reputation of at least a minor celebrity during his stay in the hospital and visits afterwards. He was a local boy, one whose feats the Orange County newspapers publicized frequently. Word of his presence spread among the hospital personnel, mostly through off-hand remarks over coffee in the cafeteria. "That's Jimmy Caruthers."

"Who?"

"Jimmy Caruthers. You know, the race driver."

"Oh yes. I think I've heard of him."

Several members of the hospital staff were more sports-oriented than others and relished their occasional encounters with Jimmy. One such person was X-ray technician Joe Aldenhifer, who enjoyed automobiles, subscribed to racing publications, and drove a Corvette. He also participated in amateur sports car events—slaloms, rallies, and tours. To Aldenhifer, Jimmy Caruthers was a person for whom dream had become reality, an honest-to-God racer, one who actually competed with the big boys.

When Jimmy visited the X-ray unit and sat around waiting for his negatives to develop, Aldenhifer frequently talked with him. Jimmy Caruthers did not always get on easily with strangers. Despite his effusiveness at the racetrack and his love of practical jokes, Jimmy was a private person, a bit of an introvert, who did not betray his feelings openly to outsiders because he worried about their reactions to him as a race driver. He had no such hang-ups with Aldenhifer, however.

On one trip to the X-ray room, he talked to Aldenhifer about money. Jimmy worried whether Clint Brawner could obtain the financing necessary for him to become competitive with the top racers. He told Joe that his race car was then three years old. "We're limited," he admitted. "We can buy the pieces we need, and keeping going to races, and pay salaries, and motel bills, and gas, and so forth. But we can't afford to buy new equipment. It's a matter of either running these old cars of Clint's or not being in the race. We're definitely not well financed. You have to lay out thirty or forty grand to buy a new race car, and we don't have the money right now to run good. Maybe Brawner can come up with some more money, or maybe I will go with another team."

Jimmy continued expostulating about his sport: "We just passed through an era. The days when a mechanic like Brawner could lay out four pieces of tubing on the floor of a shop, weld it together, put an engine on it, build a body, and take it to the racetrack and be competitive are gone forever. To go to the racetrack today, you need a mechanical engineer who can design the suspension, an aerodynamics engineer to design the body and wings, then you need a highly skilled craftsman to put the machine together."

"I wish you luck," said Aldenhifer. He looked forward

to Jimmy's visits because it gave him an inside peek at the world of auto racing.

Others in the hospital also took an interest in Jimmy. After Dr. Callaghan mended his leg, placing pins in the ankle, he told Jimmy to report daily for physiotherapy. "You need to strengthen your muscles if you want to recover in time to race at Ontario," the doctor explained.

Paul Pursell served as supervisor of the physiotherapy department at Tustin Community Hospital. He sometimes had problems convincing patients they should do rehabilitation exercises; he had no problems motivating Jimmy Caruthers. He noticed how feverishly Jimmy worked to get back in shape. It was obvious to Pursell that Jimmy wanted to return to racing as soon as possible, that nothing would get in his way, and he would do anything to speed up the system.

"I wish all my patients were as eager as you," Pursell told him one day while Jimmy was exercising on a weight machine.

Jimmy smiled: "This is my job. If I can't race, I don't eat."

Pursell thought Jimmy typical of the race drivers he met in his work. All of them were very aggressive and extremely agitated in the hospital. Their first and only desire was to get back in their cars or on their motorcycles. Jimmy fit that picture. Gabelich, Hiss, Snow, Caruthers—all were carefree and highly competitive individuals, always living fast and hard.

Paul Pursell did not follow auto racing as did Joe Aldenhifer, but like most physical therapists, he had a basic interest in sports. After becoming acquainted with Jimmy, he began watching auto racing with more interest, as did many others at Tustin Community. The following May, during broadcasts of the Indy 500, hospital personnel would work with their ears half on the radio because they wondered how their former patient was doing.

At the end of August Jimmy reported to Ontario Motor Speedway to practice for the California 500. He wore a protective boot and support. USAC officials frowned at the arrangement and decided he must pass a test before receiving permission to practice. So before their watchful eyes, Jimmy bounced in and out of the race car to demonstrate his maneuverability. "We want to be sure the cast on your leg won't inhibit your movements," explained one official.

"I understand," said Jimmy.

"You might have to get out of the car quickly in case of another accident."

"Doesn't even hurt," said Jimmy, springing up and down on the leg.

"All right," nodded the USAC official, "but we'll be watching to make sure you have no problems."

"No sweat," said Jimmy, and walked jauntily away. He strolled around the corner and, out of sight of USAC officials, reached down and grabbed his leg. Goddam, he thought, it hurts like hell.

On race day Dr. Callaghan came to watch his patient perform. He, too, had been converted into a race fan. The doctor stopped by the pits to talk to Jimmy before the race began. Reporters asked the doctor what the normal recovery time for an injury such as the one suffered by Jimmy would be. "The average person, not well-motivated, would be out at least three months," Dr. Callaghan informed them.

"That's my doctor," said Jimmy. "The miracle man of medicine."

In the California 500 it was not Jimmy's broken leg but a water line on the cooling system of his race car that halted him. He went 171 laps, good enough to place twelfth. It capped a successful season for him in championship cars. In his first year of serious racing on the championship trail Jimmy Caruthers competed officially in five races, earning

$42,833 in prize money and scoring 415 points, twentieth place in the standings. It was a good beginning in the top league of racing, and hopefully his record would improve with experience, and if he got a better car. Two more races remained in the season following Ontario, but Brawner did not enter a car in them because of inadequate financing.

Jimmy did drive the last midget race of the season at Ascot Park, the Grand Prix on Turkey Night. "I'm going to win that race someday," he told Suzie on the telephone. "That's one of my main ambitions, other than winning Indy." He failed to achieve that goal at Ascot in 1972, but was happy anyway. Auto racing writer Joe Scalzo talked to him that night. Jimmy could not conceal his excitement. For the 1973 season a wealthy Phoenix businessman named Bob Fletcher would sponsor him on the championship trail. Brawner, being from Arizona, arranged the deal. Fletcher planned to buy Jimmy a brand new Eagle and go racing first-class. Jimmy told Scalzo, "It's going to be good to race up front again."

6

Suzie Grim always considered Indianapolis a fun city, while admitting you probably had to be connected with racing to think that. Many who made their profession racing autos, or servicing those who raced autos, lived on the west side of Indianapolis near the Speedway. Or they settled in nearby towns such as Brownsburg, Clermont, Danville. Some stayed only for the summer racing season; others lived there year round.

The most popular area for race people was immediately west of the track, on the other side of Georgetown Road and south of Crawfordsville Road. The streets here were quiet, lined with trees. The homes were old, but well maintained. Rents in apartments and rooming houses were reasonable for single drivers. Many young couples lived in the Georgetown trailer court. Shopping was good. Race people could walk to work at the track—although if it became a choice between walking two blocks and jumping in a car, they jumped in a car. That was their nature.

During the summer the drivers and their crewmen often met evenings to play softball. Their wives and girl friends sat together in the bleachers and cheered. On weekends when the race was distant and women stayed at home, they sometimes got together and watched on television. (The Indianapolis media give auto racing much more attention than do the media in other American cities.) Race people bowled together. They partied together. Once a week during the winter, when the drivers played poker, their wives went to the movies together. When one of their group died, they mourned together.

It was a community of people, almost a subculture, with the same profession and with the same interests. It was a community that welcomed outsiders grudgingly because few outsiders comprehended what it was like to be a racer. An outsider attending one of their parties soon became bored. There was only one topic of conversation. Not schools, or kids, or the latest novel. Only racing.

Jimmy Caruthers loved Indianapolis as much as Suzie. He still considered himself a Californian because he had roots there, too, but he loved returning to Indianapolis each spring. It was the center of his desires. He enjoyed life there.

When not tinkering with his pickup truck, Jimmy often drove to Morris Reservoir on the northeast side of Indianapolis with drivers Pancho Carter and Johnny Parsons, Jr., to go skiing. On another day he wandered over to Dave Laycock's shop near Danville, where Gene Romero kept his motorcycle. Jimmy sat around the shop drinking beer, chattering with Burritto, and cycling in the fields out back. Billy Vukovich and Gary Bettenhausen often fished in the pond next to Laycock's, but although Jimmy occasionally did the same, he found that sport too contemplative for his tastes.

Perhaps half of those who made their homes in Indianapolis during the summer race season left town in late

September and returned to their other homes in Texas, Arizona, or California to continue racing through the winter. In January some returned briefly for the USAC banquet and a pair of midget races in Fort Wayne, then fled again to warmer climates until spring, the time to prepare for the Indianapolis 500, the pivotal event around which their lives revolved.

Jimmy migrated back and forth each year, wintering in Southern California. He no longer stayed with his mother in Anaheim, but shared an apartment in nearby La Palma with Gene Romero. He and Burritto had a working arrangement—Jimmy stayed with Gene while on the West Coast and Gene stayed with Jimmy and Suzie while in the Midwest. Suzie sometimes joked, "I agreed to live with you, not with you and Romero." During the winter of 1973 she remained in Indianapolis, continuing with her secretarial job at Hoosier Solvents & Chemicals.

Back in California, rooming with Burritto, Jimmy kept in touch with his Midwest friends by telephone. He often called long distance on impulse. One time he and Burritto came home following a party and telephoned Johnny Rutherford in Fort Worth, Texas, in the middle of the night, awakening him with a loud and cheery greeting: "Hi Johnny, what are you doing?"

Soon afterward Rutherford arose at 7:30 A.M. one morning to go to work and decided to call Jimmy Caruthers. Because of the two-hour time difference, it was 5:30 A.M. in California. Jimmy groped for the jangling telephone and pulled it to his ear. "*Mmmrrrrmmmph,*" he mumbled into the receiver.

"Hi, Jimmy. What are you doing?" came the loud and cherry greeting. After that, Johnny Rutherford received no more late calls from Jimmy Caruthers.

Whenever Jimmy was away from Suzie, he called her daily, sometimes several times daily. Or she called him. It was not uncommon for one month's telephone bill to exceed three hundred dollars.

Suzie never dated anyone else after they began living together. Since they were not married, she never extracted any promises of fidelity from Jimmy. She felt drivers' wives who kept questioning their husbands about what they did while out of town were only asking for trouble.

He returned to Indianapolis in mid December so they could spend Christmas together. He had purchased an ancient red Volkswagen on whose side he painted the number one-and-a-half. He and Suzie referred to it as the Red Baron. Jimmy never used the car for normal driving, but only as one of his many toys. Pancho Carter and Johnny Parsons, Jr., had similar junk cars. During the summer they drove the cars in a wooded area nicknamed Wounded Knee, sliding in the dirt, sometimes bouncing off each other. During the winter they moved their demolition derbies to Laycock's ice-covered pond, or the snow-packed parking lot of the 500 Shopping Center across the street from the Speedway.

Jimmy devised an injection system for the Red Baron's engine. An electric switch on the dash enabled him to spray pure nitromethane into the carburetor, causing the battered Volkswagen to leap forward like a horse spurred in the ribs.

Suzie rode shotgun during many of these impromptu races and always felt the other drivers aimed at her door during collisions. Eventually the Red Baron expired from excessive abuse. Jimmy towed it to the junk yard and went on to buy another toy.

He possessed a natural mechanical aptitude. He loved tinkering with machines. Yet he never had what some drivers referred to as a "sanitary" race car, one that sparkled in the sunlight from the care lavished on its finish by some drivers. He might spend two days working on a torsion arm bushing to assure its proper fit, but he never wasted much energy in polishing the race car. Jimmy's method of cleaning his midget racer had been to take it to an automatic car wash. He devoted considerably more attention to his truck. He owned what may have been the only $30,000 1967 Chevy pickup in the world.

Jimmy once nearly totaled the pickup, crashing in the fog, returning from the Ontario Motor Speedway. For several months the truck lay broken and abandoned outside his father's shop in Anaheim. One day Jimmy had nothing to do, so he decided to rebuild it.

When Jimmy Caruthers became involved in a project, he knew or cared about nothing else until he finished that project, or got bored with it. For nearly a month he devoted every spare minute to the pickup truck. He bought trick rods, pistons, manifolds, spending nearly two thousand dollars on the engine. He pounded out dents, straightened the frame, and repainted the body a bright yellow that threatened the California sun. The drive train (when replaced) had 200,000 miles on it, but the pickup looked, and ran, like it had just come off a Detroit assembly line. He installed an independent power source under the hood for running electrical tools and owned a citizen's band radio long before the general public discovered CBs.

He had a million toys—radio-operated planes, go-carts, jet-skis, and more different motorcycles than you could count, including street bikes, trail bikes, minibikes, even one bicycle on which he mounted a two-horsepower Briggs engine. One time during the month of May David Clutter, M.D., the assistant medical director at the Speedway, stopped by Gasoline Alley with a friend and introduced him to Jimmy. Dr. Clutter's friend noticed Jimmy's motorized bicycle and remarked that he owned a similar one. Jimmy spent the next two hours with the man discussing how their motorbikes worked.

* * *

Jimmy looked forward to the 1973 season because of Clint Brawner's success in locating an honest-to-God, first-class, bucks-up backer, one reportedly not afraid to go racing first-class. Bob Fletcher was a Phoenix businessman and gentleman farmer whose Fletcher Enterprises covered a cornucopia of businesses from selling automotive parts to supplying equipment for Arizona's copper mines. Fletcher also operated a chain of tire companies which he called Cobre Tires (*cobre* coming from the Spanish word for copper). A car nut as a boy, he attended the Indy 500 for the first time in 1972, and decided that, at age fifty-two, if he ever planned to get involved in racing at Indy, it had better be soon. Besides, it would be good advertising for his many auto-related businesses.

When Fletcher decided to go racing at Indy, he turned to Clint as a fellow Arizonian, hiring him as crew chief. Brawner brought along as driver his protégé, Jimmy Caruthers. Fletcher supplied the newly founded Fletcher Racing team with two new Eagle race cars painted the Fletcher racing colors, copper and turquoise (turquoise being frequently found in copper mines).

Before Fletcher signed Jimmy Caruthers as number one driver on his team, Jimmy flew into Phoenix to discuss contractual arrangements. He arrived at Fletcher's office wearing pink pants and a wildly colored shirt. Fletcher took one look at him and asked, "Do the other members of the band have that same uniform?"

Jimmy laughed and Fletcher laughed, and the others in the office laughed. After that the businessman and the driver seemed to get along well. "Sure, send along the papers," said Jimmy after they discussed money. "I'll sign." Fletcher offered Jimmy a three-year contract providing a guaranteed base salary of $14,000 a year plus expenses and the usual 40 percent cut of his prize money. More important than dollar signs and percentage points to Jimmy was Fletcher's promise to provide him with first-class equipment and support. That was what it took to win Indy.

Jimmy soon developed almost a family relationship with Bob Fletcher and his wife. Jimmy, about the same age as Fletcher's oldest son, used to kid Bob Fletcher's wife, calling her "Ma Fletcher," or sometimes "Grandmaw." Mrs. Fletcher sometimes asked her husband, "Well, how's my boy today?" meaning Jimmy.

Bob Fletcher worried about Jimmy's motorcycle riding, fearing he might fall off and get hurt. "Why do you ride those things?" asked Fletcher one day.

"It's how I keep in shape," Jimmy alibied.

"Why don't you lift weights instead, or run two or three miles a day? That way there's no danger of breaking a leg."

"Don't worry, Bob," Jimmy told his owner, a wide grin on his face. "If that happens, I know a good doctor." He kept on riding his motorcycle.

Although it had not begun that way, Fletcher began to consider his move into auto racing as somewhat of a crusade. He expressed to reporters his philosophy that if auto racing were to prosper, young drivers such as Jimmy Caruthers must be brought along to replace veterans like Foyt, Andretti, and the Unsers.

Jimmy, however, took a more realistic approach as to why it was difficult for young drivers such as himself to nudge older drivers aside. "Racing is safer now than it was twenty years ago," he said. "We're killing fewer drivers."

Bob Fletcher was a religious man. He did not drink, did not smoke, and did not care for others doing it around him. He neither allowed beer in his garages nor permitted smoking on his private airplane. The only one who seemed able to break those rules was Jimmy Caruthers. He would light a cigarette while flying to a race or walk into the garage, a can of Coors in his hand, and say to Bob, "What's happening?" Fletcher seemed to tolerate his young driver's peccadillos as he might tolerate those of a favorite, but wayward, son.

Fletcher felt uncomfortable, however, about Jimmy's living openly with Suzie Grim. He said nothing, but it displeased him and his wife.

Success did not come instantly for the Fletcher Racing Team. It rarely does. Usually with any new combination it takes a while before people begin communicating with each other. New equipment, while preferable to old equipment, often is unreliable until the mechanics figure out how it works. Jimmy dropped out of the first championship car race in Texas in April after thirty laps because of clutch failure. The following weekend in Trenton, New Jersey, low oil pressure sidelined him after eighty-three laps. In May the Indianapolis Motor Speedway opened for practice.

Indianapolis, for those in the racing fraternity, may be a fun city eleven months a year, but not during the month of May. Too much tension is involved as drivers and crew prepare for what is the single most important event of the year—the Indianapolis 500.

Partly it is the money. Speedway owner Tony Hulman offers a pot of more than a million dollars in prizes. The winning team usually earns in excess of $250,000. A car that merely makes the field and finishes thirty-third gets close to $15,000. The driver's share usually comes to 40 percent of the winnings, plus bonuses and salary. His ability to negotiate favorable future contracts with better percentages, better bonuses, and a better salary often depends upon his record at Indianapolis.

Partly it is the crowds. No other sporting event in the United States attracts such a huge audience. Several thousand people drop by the track each day just to watch practice. Two hundred thousand people appear for "Pole day," the first day of qualifications. Three hundred thousand come to the race itself. More than a hundred million listen to the live radio broadcast featuring Sid Collins. Thirty million watch the delayed telecast later that night on ABC. Additional millions all over the world read about the results the following day.

Partly it is the spectacle. It is the parade, the parties, the playing of "On the Wabash," the singing of "Back Home Again in Indiana," the balloons in the air, the sight of Tony Hulman standing in the back of the pace car, saying into the microphone, "Gentlemen, start your engines," the cheer that follows, the roar of the engines, the pace car leading the field once, then twice, around the two-and-a-half-mile track, then ducking into the pits, the flash of the green flag signaling the race's start, and the explosion of sound as thirty-three cars race down the front straightaway aimed at the first turn. It is probably the single most exciting moment in sport, yet many in that crowd of three hundred thousand avert their eyes. They find themselves unable to look into that first turn, so great is the tension at that moment.

Partly it is the tradition. Indianapolis has more than sixty years of history. There is knowledge on the part of each of the thirty-three drivers that should fate smile on him and allow the mantle of victory to fall over his shoulders, he will win not only fortune, he will win fame, lasting respect as an Indy winner, something to carry with him the rest of his life, wherever he goes. Each Christmas Speedway owner Tony Hulman distributes a set of four matched glasses to friends of racing. The glasses vary only slightly from year to year, the main difference being one more addition to the list of Indy 500 winners embossed on the side. It is the ambition of every race driver to have his name on Tony Hulman's Christmas glasses.

It was the ambition of Jimmy Caruthers to have his name on those glasses. "I'm going to win the big one someday," he kept telling Jerry McClung during all those miles of travel over the roads of the Midwest from race to race, from track to track. And after Jerry quit coming to the Midwest, he informed other close friends of that burning desire that was so vital a part of his life. Yet in an interview with a reporter from the *Wall Street Journal,* he tried to downplay the importance of the Indy 500, saying that to condition himself mentally for the race he attempted to shoo all the glitter from his mind. "You can really get psyched out by this place," Jimmy explained. "That happened to me as a rookie and I stumbled around in a big daze. Now I try to forget this place is special. When the engines start, I don't know there is anyone else here."

In speaking to the reporter, however, Jimmy Caruthers probably overstated his cool. He was aware of the glitter; it was impossible not to be. He focused his mind almost entirely on the race during the month of May and became very introverted. They never went to parties in May. They usually stayed home. Jimmy did not like public speaking in May. Usually he and Suzie would eat dinner, watch television, and go to bed early. He rarely went out drinking with the other drivers during May. He saved that for the other eleven months of the year.

There exists another dimension to Indy that everyone knows is there but hesitates to speak about—the threat of death. Auto racing is like a black widow spider that devours its mate. Long is the list of those who loved and lost.

Jimmy Caruthers knew that every time he stepped into a race car he might die. He and Suzie talked about it frequently. He did not anticipate that dying would be a traumatic experience. He was not afraid to die. If he had to die at the age of twenty-eight, or twenty-nine, or thirty, he would die knowing he had lived more in those twenty-eight, twenty-nine, or thirty years than most people live in sixty, seventy, or eighty years. That was the way he expressed it to her.

Suzie, in her love for Jimmy, also prepared herself for
the fact that, as she put it, "something terrible might happen to him in a race car." She was not frightened because
she considered herself a fatalist—what will be, will be. She
was ready to accept their fate.

That did not mean she would like it.

In the meantime she purchased a mail subscription to
the Indianapolis *Star* for the month of May, having the
newspaper sent each day to Jimmy's mother back in Anaheim. She also sent her flowers on Mother's Day, knowing
Jimmy would never think of that. Suzie felt that even
though Jimmy's mother would not come to the Indy 500,
would not even watch its delayed telecast, she was still interested in what her son was doing. She thought it would
be nice if his mother knew. She was disappointed when
Jimmy's mother never thanked her for her attention.

At the end of April Bob Fletcher decided to add another
driver to his racing team—Art Pollard. Pollard competed
in the first race of the season in Texas for STP's racing
team, but his chances of getting a good car from STP at
Indy seemed chancy. STP's Andy Granatelli hired as his
crew chief George Bignotti, whose cars had won more
championship races than any other mechanic's. Bignotti
had new Eagles for his drivers, Gordon Johncock and
Swede Savage. Granatelli offered a new Lola to Pollard,
but Art disliked the car and did not relish having to wait
for Bignotti to make a spare Eagle available after his top
two drivers qualified. When Bob Fletcher asked Pollard to
drive for him, Pollard accepted.

Jimmy Caruthers was delighted to be teamed with Art
Pollard again. Clint Brawner, however, had misgivings
since Pollard brought with him his chief mechanic, Ron
Falk. Although the cars of both Caruthers and Pollard
were entered under the name of Fletcher Racing, they had
separate (although adjoining) garages in Gasoline Alley.
The two teams practiced independently of each other.

Brawner and Falk did not communicate easily, and if new parts arrived, an argument often ensued as to who got first pick. Usually Art Pollard served as mediator.

After several days of practice, Pollard began running extremely fast because Falk accidentally stumbled across the trick to make the new Eagles handle well, known by only a few other teams. While looking through an album of photographs taken by Dennis Torres, he noticed that their front wings bent downward in the turns. He decided they could not function aerodynamically as effectively in a flexed position and increased the support on the wings by substituting heavier tubing.

In practice the next day Pollard increased his speed from 184 to 188 miles per hour. He came in beaming, "That's the tip."

The stiffer wing increased the Eagle's stability through the turns and eliminated its main handling problem—unpredictability. Falk later examined photographs of other fast cars and noticed their wings also remained stable. Falk suggested Art mention their discovery to Jimmy. Jimmy, in turn, suggested the change to Clint. Brawner accepted the advice grudgingly. The piece of heavy tubing sat in a corner of the garage for three days before Jimmy complained enough to get it installed. His times immediately improved.

Jimmy Caruthers and Art Pollard became close friends. The disparity in their ages proved no barrier. The two worked together and played together. Sometimes while their cars were being repaired they played golf on the nine-hole golf course in the middle of the racetrack.

Golf bored Jimmy. After a few holes it became a game of not how few strokes you used, but how fast you went from tee to green. He hit the ball, raced his cart to where it landed, hit again, then raced on, sometimes not bothering to pick up the golf ball. Sand traps were a hazard only in that you might tip your cart over bouncing through them.

Art helped Jimmy with his racing, and Jimmy looked to him for advice. He did not need much coaching on how to drive a race car, but when he did need to learn something, he knew Art would tell him the truth.

Sometimes the two drivers sat around and talked. Sometimes the talk got serious, like one evening after practice when they stopped off for a beer. "Knowing what happened to Danny," Art asked once, "if you had to do it all over again, would you still race?"

"You mean even if I knew Danny was going to get snuffed?"

"Right."

The noise in the bar where they stopped was intense. But the silence between them was also intense. Finally Jimmy broke it: "I'd still race."

Art shook his head. "I don't know," he said morosely. "I sometimes wonder myself about this crazy profession of ours. I've been hurt a little, but I've never been hurt real bad. I don't know what I'd do if I ever got hurt bad."

Jimmy said nothing. He knew what Art meant.

Pollard continued, "Now and then I wonder if I wouldn't be just as happy back home in Medford, Oregon, working in the Chevrolet garage again. Before I got involved with all this Indy business, I was already into my thirties and had established a total life back in that small town. I raced for fun on the weekends and went back to work on Monday mornings and wrote orders for servicing cars. I was a fixture in town, like the local barber, the local insurance man. Everybody who owned a Chevy and went into that garage knew me."

Pollard paused as though amazed of his own awareness. He grimaced. "And here I am in the middle of my life, riding all over the country on jet airplanes, eating in expensive restaurants, doing what race drivers do. I'm not dissatisfied, but it's just so totally different. Once I raced each weekend for fun, and now I race with my tail in a sling. I don't know. I just don't know."

By Wednesday the week before qualifications began Art Pollard consistently practiced at speeds above 190 miles per hour. He looked certain to qualify near the front of the pack. Many teams come to Indy and spend all month trying to catch up, but Falk and Pollard had their car running smoothly with time to spare. They had no worries about making the show. They now had the luxury of several days in which they could attempt small adjustments to the chassis, or the wings, or the amount of turbocharger boost, any one of which might allow them to squeeze an extra bit of speed out of their car. And Pollard could refine his skills on a track which, despite its apparent simplicity, is one of the world's most difficult to drive.

Indy is difficult because it is simple, because there are so few things a driver can do to improve his speed. It is a fine track, a precise track, and one on which the margin of error is exacting because of the tremendous speeds on the straightaways and through the turns. One slight miscalculation, hanging it out a fraction over the fine line, and the driver careens into the wall, destroying perhaps both machine and himself. But unless he runs right on that fine line, he will never achieve success at Indy.

It is often the very fast drivers who tend to lose control more than the slower drivers. They know the only way to go faster is to hang it out a little more. They have more confidence. They know, or think, that no matter how far out they get, they can save it. And they are right in one sense: They must feel that way or they will never win.

On Saturday morning a gusty wind out of the southwest blew across the straightaway. Drivers fear winds because they add another element of unpredictability to their jobs. Particularly at Indy, winds can be tricky, swirling in and around the grandstands and blowing debris across the track. Early in the morning Art Pollard practiced with eighty-eight inches of boost on the turbocharger blowing fuel into his engine. This was less than the ninety-two to ninety-four inches he had been practicing with during the week. He and his mechanic did not want to turn the boost too high, as some mechanics do on pole day, and risk blowing their engine. But Pollard came in after several laps, wanting more boost, so Falk turned it up to ninety inches.

Pollard restarted his engine and drove slowly down the pit row and out onto the track. It takes nearly a full lap of the two-and-a-half-mile track at Indy for drivers to reach full speed. Pollard came around the first time moving fast. Ron Falk, standing on the grass at the edge of the track, started his stopwatch. Back in the pits Clint Brawner and his crew worked on Jimmy Caruthers' car. Jimmy sat on the pit wall nearby, waiting for his turn to practice, anxious to get going.

At that moment the yellow light went on, indicating a problem on the track. Falk looked down the long straightaway to where Pollard had passed out of sight. Grandstands blocked his view of all but the start of the turn. Falk saw nothing. He stopped his stopwatch, since the yellow light meant Pollard would have to slow down and come in before completion of the lap. A USAC official wearing earphones stood nearby. The official turned to Falk: "Ron, it's Art."

The USAC official said no more immediately, and since Falk heard no crash, he assumed Pollard probably shut off and coasted into the infield grass, where a tow truck would pick him up and bring him in. It happens all the time at Indy during practice, usually for minor problems. But Falk worried because the problem might delay their qualifying. Then the USAC official said, "The car is on fire."

On the far side of the track in turn two Pollard's race car lay upside down, a twisted clump of metal, totally unrecognizable as a piece of automotive machinery, an object of avant-garde art, a creation of modern man at his worst, with Art Pollard lying in the wreckage, unconscious.

Watching from the field hospital located in the infield was the Speedway's assistant medical director, David Clutter, M.D., a close friend of Art and his wife. Dr. Clutter saw the car hit, go upside down, and erupt into flames, so he knew somebody was going to be coming in hurt, but he did not know who.

Finally they brought the driver in, and it was Art. He was unconscious. He was burned significantly on the hands, feet, and face, everywhere the uniform broke. He was not breathing well, and as soon as he arrived at the hospital his heart stopped. Dr. Clutter had to shock him to restart the heart, then had trouble forcing air down into his chest past his burned esophagus. A surgeon arrived and put a chest tube in him.

While this desperate effort to save Art Pollard's life continued, Ron Falk waited outside the field hospital. He arrived in time to see Art carried in from the ambulance and noticed, with some relief, that he did not look seriously hurt. He had burns on the neck and on the arm, but Falk had seen much worse. But when the doctors continued working on his driver, Falk got the feeling that it was pretty bad. The field hospital placed Pollard in an ambulance for transport to Methodist Hospital downtown. Falk climbed in a car to follow.

When he arrived at Methodist Hospital, Falk learned Art Pollard was dead. He had broken his neck when his car struck upside down. All the massive medical attempt to save him was futile. Falk climbed back in his truck and returned to the track. He could not think of anywhere better to go. In Gasoline Alley the tow truck crew had slid Art's broken race car into the garage. Clint Brawner was next door. When Falk walked in, Clint asked, "How is he?"

"We lost him," said Falk.

Clint grimaced and turned away.

After Art's accident Jimmy Caruthers drove to the section of the Speedway where his friend died. He drove through turns one and two because he wanted to find out how Art Pollard died. He also wanted to know if there was some danger to himself because he drove a similar race car.

He examined the skid marks on the track surface. He talked to a number of observers on those turns and asked them what happened, what they had seen. He got varying replies. A few observers thought it might be a case of driver error—what Art himself used to laugh and call "brain drain." Others suggested a gust of wind might have upset the downforces on the car's rear wing as it passed the alley between the main grandstand and the next grandstand. Nobody wanted to speculate on whether or not some part on the race car broke.

Jimmy examined the remnants of the race car, the shattered shell. It had been so brutally ripped apart that for all Jimmy knew, some gangster might have wired the car with dynamite.

After he finished making his inquiries and examinations, Jimmy Caruthers returned to the pits and climbed into a car almost identical to the one driven by Art Pollard and qualified for the Indianapolis 500.

It was very quiet in the pits the remainder of that day. It always gets quiet in the pits around a racetrack after somebody gets hurt. Nobody talks. The least said, the better is the attitude of most race people. They look at each other, then look away. They know what happened, but they do not mention what happened. They communicate by their silence.

What could anyone say? The most appropriate comment was inscribed on a cigarette lighter Jimmy carried in the pocket of his driver's uniform: "Fuck it! Just fuck it!"

A number of people said it took great courage on the part of Jimmy Caruthers, nerves of steel, and indifference toward fate, maybe even a certain callousness, for him to climb into a race car and qualify within hours of his teammate's death. They saw him walk away from the pits after qualifying. They saw him, unsmiling, cold, seemingly without emotion. They saw him climb onto his motorcycle to ride with Suzie back to their apartment. What they did not see was what happened when he got back to that apartment. He cried.

"I didn't want to get in that race car," he told her, tears streaming down his cheeks.

"You did it, Jim," said Suzie, putting an arm over his shoulder. "You did it."

"But damn it, I didn't want to!"

They sat silent for a while. For a moment Suzie wondered what she would do if someday Jimmy's life ended like that of Art Pollard's. But before she could come up with an answer, she put the thought out of her mind.

It would get more quiet at Indianapolis, much more quiet. Two weeks later on race day, Jimmy rode to the track, Suzie on the back of his motorcycle. It was raining and Suzie got soaked. The rain stopped, the track dried, and the race began, but even before the lead cars reached the first turn, disaster struck. Two cars bounced off each other, spun, and soon half a dozen cars went spinning down the track, one of them with its fuel tanks ruptured, spraying flames into the grandstand seats. When the smoke cleared, Salt Walther's car was most severely damaged and he was most severely injured, his legs dangling out the front of the broken shell of a race car. At least he survived.

It rained again even before the debris could be swept from the track. The track dried, and it rained again. Eventually everybody went home. It rained again the next day, Tuesday, causing more delay, the first double postponement in 500 history. The drivers became more and more tense.

Jimmy Caruthers rarely slept the night before a big race. He usually went to bed only to toss and turn. He got up, smoked a cigarette, went to the toilet, sat in the living room, smoked another cigarette, had a drink of water, tried to sleep again, and failed. You cannot easily go to sleep without closing your eyes and Jimmy Caruthers could not close his eyes. He lay in bed, eyes open, looking ahead to the next day. It was not so much the fear of death, or the thought of all that fame and fortune awaiting him if he got it together. It was just Indianapolis. Indianapolis is Indianapolis, and it is never fun for drivers in the month of May.

It rained again Wednesday morning, but finally the skies cleared and the race began.

Suzie had a seat in Tower Terrace on the inside of the track near the entrance to the pits. Jimmy's father sat there, too, as did his new wife, Dana. Doug recently had married Dana Ward, who had previously been married to Rodger Ward, Jr. Sitting with them was Jimmy's younger sister, Deed, at the Indy 500 for the first time since her brother Danny's death. Most of the wives and families of the drivers occupied the same section in Tower Terrace, their seats reserved for them by the Speedway management.

The crowd, those few who remained after two days of rain, rose for the start. When the cars negotiated the first turn without incident and came rushing past at the end of lap one, the crowd sighed in relief. As lap piled upon lap, the cars spread out in a long line, and the crowd settled in their seats. After a while the drivers started coming in for their first pit stops, and there was a flurry of excitement as everyone rose again to see who would emerge the leader.

Several drivers already retired from the race, their cars beset by mechanical problems.

The race continued, and the crowd relaxed, content with its role as witness of history. They reached into coolers for cans of beer and pieces of Kentucky Fried Chicken and waited for the inevitable decision as to who would emerge winner of the Indy 500 that year and be remembered with the other immortals of auto racing. A frisbee was being thrown in the infield.

Suddenly, almost before anyone noticed it, one of the cars spun out of control. Coming out of the fourth turn and into the front straightaway, the car veered left and shot toward the inside retaining wall. It struck with a tremendous impact, exploding into a red ball of flame. The sound of the explosion echoed among screams from the crowd. There was little question in the minds of anyone witnessing the ferocity of the crash—the driver of that car had to be dead.

A wave of terror struck the drivers' families seated in Tower Terrace. The accident occurred just down the track from where they sat. The smoke from the fire spread out toward them, burning their eyes and causing them to catch their breath. They were so close as to be almost part of the tragedy. Yet the car was so severely damaged that nobody could tell whose it had been!

Action on the track ceased almost instantly. The starter waved the red flag, temporarily halting the race. A few drivers came into the pits. Most stopped their cars at points around the track, many at the head of the straightaway, others on the back stretch. The wives seated in Tower Terrace anxiously began looking up and down the track, hoping for some sign that it was not their husband killed before their eyes. Sirens began to wail.

Joy Snider began screaming hysterically. She realized the car was red. Her husband, George Snider, drove a red car and she thought it was he. Wavelyn Bettenhausen, Gary's wife, began crying. Her father-in-law had been killed at Indianapolis. Her brother-in-law had had an arm ripped from his body in another driving accident. Now she believed her husband had met death. The wife of one driver already dead, Pat Pollard, rose from her seat and stoically began walking down the stairs to leave the grandstands. Accompanying her was Cheryl Savage, wife of driver Swede Savage, who already knew the identity of the driver in the wreck.

Deed Caruthers could not halt the tears streaming down her face. Her brother, Jimmy, had not come around. She could not see his car. She knew it was him. Her father also thought it might have been Jimmy. Doug tried to focus his field glasses on the wreck, but his hands were shaking so badly that he could not hold them steady. He finally focused on the wreck, but still could not tell whose car it was.

Suzie Grim sat silently in the stands, betraying no emotion. Immediately after the impact, Mary Ann Simon, wife of driver Dick Simon, collapsed into her lap. She still was bent over, softly sobbing. Although Suzie seemed calm, a scene from another race seven years earlier flashed through her mind. The year was 1966 and she was sixteen at the time, seated in almost the identical place, next to her mother. Bobby Grim was racing on the track. It was still lap one, and as the lead cars came out of the fourth turn, a multicar accident occurred with her father caught in the middle. As the race cars of Eddie Sachs and Dave MacDonald slid, burning, down the banked turn, Suzie became hysterical. Her actual father died in a stock car race before she could remember him; she feared her second father, whom she knew and loved, would also be stolen from her. She screamed. Her mother slapped Suzie in the face. "Don't you ever do that again," she said. "I've got enough problems of my own without you getting upset." As it happened, her father was not injured, although Sachs and

MacDonald died. Afterwards, Suzie Grim tried never to let her emotions show.

She carried with her a portable radio because she liked to listen to the broadcast of the 500 while watching it. Announcer Sid Collins soon began mentioning the names of drivers he and observers could spot still on the track, trying to identify the victim by elimination. The track announcer began doing the same. Both finally said that Jimmy Caruthers stopped his car safely on the other side of the track.

Neither the Speedway management nor Sid Collins identified the driver in the crash, although by now they knew. In the press box reporters angrily telephoned Collins for information. "It isn't official," Collins replied. "I can't tell you until it's official." Several reporters became so angry that they threatened to cross the track and punch Collins in the nose.

Doug Caruthers decided to walk toward the scene of the accident, but could not get close because of the crowds. Eventually he spotted Wayne Leary, Bobby Unser's mechanic, returning along the grass toward the pits. "It was Swede," Larry said.

While the attention of most of the spectators was focused on the accident involving Swede Savage, another tragedy occurred directly in front of the families in Tower Terrace. Armando Toran, a pit crewman for driver Graham McRae, ran toward the accident scene and stepped into the path of a speeding fire engine, one traveling the wrong way down what normally was the one-way pit road. The fire engine struck Toran and flipped him in the air. He was dead before he hit the ground. Dr. Clutter, who examined Armando Toran in the field hospital, said that hardly a bone in the mechanic's body was not broken.

Swede Savage, however, remained alive, though incredibly burned. Ambulance attendants lifted him out of his wrecked car and took him to Methodist Hospital. The race resumed—and Jimmy Caruthers nearly became the Speedway's fourth victim that year. Wally Dallenbach's engine exploded on the front straightaway. Several laps later, Jimmy ran over a piece of debris from Dallenbach's engine, slashing his right front tire. It was an incident similar to what caused his accident the previous summer at Pocono.

Jimmy found himself rushing down the front straightaway, aimed at the first turn on only three wheels. The car began shaking and jostling and Jimmy felt his heart beating stronger as he fought to maintain a straight line.

Luck, however, rode with him. When the tire exploded, a piece of rubber hit the right wing, knocking it off. The change in aerodynamics caused the right side of the car to lift. Jimmy found himself able to steer with the left wheel. He worried about getting the car turned before reaching the corner, but slowed in time and stopped in the infield. He had not finished the race, but he had survived.

Liquor flows freely around the Speedway during the month of May. In the infield many of the spectators come not to watch the race, but to be part of the event: to sit in their campers, to watch the pretty girls, to throw their frisbees, and get drunk. Walk through the infield before the race and you find many people lying on blankets in the grass, already passed out. The parties are more respectable in the hospitality suites which rent for $10,000 annually in the Speedway Motel's annex above turn two. People drink martinis instead of beer, don't throw frisbees, and don't pass out until they get to their own rooms. There are additional parties in the homes of racing people on the west side, rousing, noisy parties that sometimes go all night. Many of the drivers visit the suites, stop by the homes, then by 8:00 appear at the Meridian Street studios of the local ABC affiliate to watch the delayed telecast of the race, usually blacked out in Indianapolis. But while parties went ahead on schedule after the race in 1973, they were more subdued. While many of the drivers got drunk, on schedule, it was not as a release from the month-long tension, but because they wanted to blot out what happened. The race won that year by Gordon Johncock was best forgotten quickly.

Jimmy and Suzie attended no parties that year. Jimmy Caruthers showed no interest in getting drunk. Instead, he went with Suzie to Methodist Hospital and sat with Cheryl Savage and Swede's parents. There was not much they could say, but at least they could be present. Within the cold, sterile walls of a room in Methodist Hospital Swede Savage lay dying, badly burned, his body shattered. It would take more than a week before the end finally came, before his kidneys failed, but he already was a terminal case and few among those who waited outside had much hope.

Jimmy and Suzie sat off in a corner together. He stared at her for a long time, saying nothing, his eyes focused on hers, trying to peer into her mind. "I'm not sure you love me," he finally said, almost in a whisper.

"I love you," Suzie insisted, equally as softly.

"I don't know."

"I do." She placed her hand in his and squeezed.

"You don't seem to show any emotions."

Suzie was silent.

Jimmy continued, "Like when everyone else was very upset, you acted as though nothing had happened."

"Yeah," admitted Suzie, laughing wryly. "That's because I took two Valiums before the race."

Jimmy raised her hand to almost under his chin. He stared down at it without saying anything. What seemed like a minute passed. "After Art died, I didn't want to get back in that race car." He paused and thought some more. He suddenly lowered her hand. "And now, I'm still not sure I want to keep going. I mean, I really could walk away and say, 'screw the whole thing.'"

Suzie squeezed his hand.

"I don't know," said Jimmy, fearfully. "Maybe I don't love racing as much as I thought I did."

"Jimmy, I'll bet there are at least thirty guys who raced today feeling the same way."

He nodded. There was another long silence.

"Well, you could," said Suzie, staring at him questioningly.

"Could what?"

"Could quit."

Jimmy nodded his head as though saying yes, but his words denied his actions. "I really don't think so."

"Why not?"

"I don't know," said Jimmy, this time shaking his head no.

"Why not live a life like a normal person?"

"Because, I guess, I'm not a normal person."

7

There was an additional loser at Indianapolis in 1973—
Clint Brawner. On the final practice day before the race
Brawner did not complete work on Jimmy's car until five
minutes before the track closed. The crew pushed the car
onto the track, but before Jimmy could drive one lap, it
quit.

Jimmy Caruthers was angry. He rarely displayed his anger to others, but he was angry at Brawner that day because he felt Clint's delay endangered their chances of
finishing high in the race.

Owner Bob Fletcher showed even more anger when he
flew into Indianapolis the following day. "There's no ex-
cuse for it," Fletcher raged at Brawner. "If you're interested in safety, you just don't do things the last minute. The
car should have been ready!" He fired Clint Brawner on
the spot.

Brawner's departure meant Jimmy would have to adjust
to a series of different chief mechanics working on his car.

Clint's nephew and assistant, Bill Brawner, became chief mechanic for the Indy 500. After that race, Red Herman took over chief mechanic chores. Plagued by a series of mid-season engine failures, Jimmy accumulated a number of sixteenth, nineteenth, and fifteenth places. Toward the end of the season he began finishing with more consistency—eighth, ninth, although he still could not run up front with the top drivers. In one qualifying heat for the California 500, he took fourth, although another engine failure forced him out of the main race.

The year proved to be one of learning for Jimmy Caruthers. He placed twenty-first in the driver standings with 408 points, earning $39,340. It was not a good year, but on the other hand it was not a bad year either. Jimmy Caruthers did not complain. He merely shook his head and said, "I hope we can be more competitive in 1974."

Before he headed west that fall, Suzie Grim told Jimmy she would like to move into larger quarters. The apartment they then shared seemed too small. "Sure," said Jimmy. "Find a new place." In December she called him in California to say she located a house within walking distance of the Speedway. It rented for $175 a month. "Sounds good," said Jimmy. So Suzie signed the lease.

When he returned to Indianapolis the next spring, Suzie had their house ready. She repainted all the rooms and bought new furniture. She converted one of the bedrooms into a trophy room, decorating it with black and white checkered curtains. She covered one wall with racing photos (of cars, crashes, and victory lane celebrations) and filled a bookcase with Jimmy's trophies. It was a minor shrine to Jimmy Caruthers, racer. As such, it was typical in many respects, and similar to trophy rooms in other racing homes on the west side of Indianapolis. It was the wives who maintained these shrines; or, in some instances, the girl friends.

Suzie also kept in the room a large scrapbook bound with black leather that included press clippings and photographs beginning with the year Jimmy won the USAC midget championship. She began collecting the clippings and photographs soon after they started dating, souvenirs of time spent together, happy times and sad times. Suzie was following the lead of her mother, who filled two scrapbooks documenting the accomplishments of Bobby Grim. One evening Jimmy had visited the Grim home for dinner and admired those books, thought they were "neat," so Suzie fashioned one almost identical and presented it to him for his birthday.

Jimmy Caruthers settled easily into the new house Suzie rented for them. He felt comfortable in it. And she felt comfortable in the house, despite their not being legally married. When she thought about it later, Suzie considered it funny that only a few years before, she had been so panic-stricken about being an old maid that she came close to marrying a boy she did not love. Now she found herself living with someone she loved, yet felt no pressure to marry. She accepted the fact that Jimmy, after his previous divorce, did not want another marriage with its accompanying restrictions.

None of their very close friends questioned their relationship, but then several of those friends had similar relationships—Gene Romero and his girl friend, Nancy; Lee Kunzman and his girl friend, Bev.

They did, on occasion, talk about marriage and they did, on occasion, talk about having children. Jimmy had one child—Jimmy Bryan Caruthers—and Suzie expressed her disappointment that that name was already taken. "We can never have a son and name him after you," she sighed one night.

"Sure we can," said Jimmy.

"But there already is a Jimmy."

"Makes no difference."

121

Suzie looked puzzled. So Jimmy explained, "You forget that my actual name is Douglas James Caruthers, Junior. I'm named after Pops. If we had a son, he could become Douglas James Caruthers the third."

Suzie beamed, "Little Dougie!"

"Well, I don't know about that," mumbled Jimmy. "I was thinking of calling him Leadfoot."

But such talk was mostly chatter. Although they talked about marriage from time to time, and about having children from time to time, and his quitting as a driver from time to time, the assumption was that these things, if they occurred, would happen far in the future. Jimmy understood that he would not race cars at Indy all his life—or even as long as some of the older drivers like Lloyd Ruby or Roger McCluskey—but he still had too many goals to fulfill before considering retirement, or marriage, or children.

Jimmy and Suzie saw their friends frequently because most were race people. They attended parties at the apartment Larry Rice shared with several bachelor friends. Or Suzie cooked Mexican food and invited Johnny and Pam Parsons over for dinner. They spent time with Suzie's parents, or with Doug and his new wife, Dana, playing a board game called "Aggravation," which Dana usually won. Doug, as was his nature, sometimes got mad and dumped the board on the floor, although Dana claimed he had calmed considerably since Danny's death. Now and then Jean Cochran, former *Playboy* playmate and model for the Hurst Gearshift Company, joined the game, as did Willie Davis, Gary Bettenhausen's mechanic.

They spent a lot of time sitting around just talking racing—remembering great races, great drivers, wondering who would be driving for which owner next year. They worried about finances—the high cost of automotive parts, the difficulty of attracting sponsors. They discussed plans for getting together and doing something after the season, like going camping in Mexico. They frequently talked about such trips, but usually, when "after the season" came, they were too busy getting ready for next season to do anything.

Jimmy and Suzie went out to dinner occasionally with friends of hers who were nonracing people, but they rarely spent much time with them.

Among their close friends practically the only ones not involved with racing were Carl Robertson and his wife. He was an Indianapolis policeman, but a race fan as well; so he fit in easily. Carl had a pontoon boat which he used for fishing on Eagle Creek Reservoir, west of Indianapolis. Jimmy sometimes went out with Carl even though the boat's maximum speed of ten miles per hour stifled him.

"Grab a pole, Jimmy," Carl told him. "The fish are getting hungry."

Jimmy grinned, "You fish for both of us, Carl. I don't have enough patience."

"Don't you like fishing?"

"If you could catch something every five minutes, it would be okay. But I don't like to wait with a pole in my hand for an hour. I'll just sit here, have a beer, and watch you fish."

"We can go in if you like."

"Oh hell no. I may not have enough patience to fish, but I've got plenty of patience to sit here and drink beer."

Jimmy Caruthers began his second season running for Fletcher with a new chief mechanic, Jim McGee. It was his fourth mechanic in two years.

When Bob Fletcher announced the establishment of his racing team to the press the previous year, he downplayed his aspirations. He announced he did not expect instant success. He expressed his belief that obtaining the proper combination of car, driver, and mechanic was something not easy to achieve overnight, that he was looking forward to long-range success. He also believed that new young drivers must be encouraged if the sport of auto racing was to prosper.

It was a fine, humble beginning. Nevertheless, after a season of racing with no victories, Bob Fletcher understandably began to have second thoughts. He started to wish that success did not have to be *quite* that long-range. Like all others who paid the bills for the championship cars, he coveted a victory at Indianapolis. He wanted to stand in victory lane at the Speedway with the camera lenses of the world focused upon him, and share with his driver that moment of glory. No one could blame Bob Fletcher for harboring such a desire.

Fletcher's introduction to big-time racing had been tragic, beginning with Art Pollard's death. After that, there had been flashes of glory, but only flashes. At Pocono in 1973 Jimmy Caruthers led the race for twenty-four laps, the first laps he ever led in a championship race. Some drivers spend entire careers in USAC without ever leading a lap at any level of racing. But a burned piston sidelined Jimmy on the hundred twenty-fourth lap.

At Ontario in March 1974 Jimmy placed second in the 100-mile qualifying heat for the California 500, then placed fourth in the race itself, his best showing in a championship car. The reporters began to visit Jimmy's pits more frequently now. "Auto racing is like a giant poker game," Jimmy told them. "We're all trying for the last big hand of the night." Judging from his progress, it seemed certain that sooner or later Jimmy Caruthers would win that big poker hand, perhaps at Indianapolis. Only one question remained—would it be soon enough to satisfy Bob Fletcher?

Racing at Phoenix the week after Ontario, Jimmy wanted to win because of all his friends in Phoenix, and because it was Bob Fletcher's hometown. On the eighth lap, however, moving into the first turn, Roger McCluskey cut beneath him. They brushed wheels. The contact knocked Jimmy up and into the wall. The crash damaged his race car, but Jimmy was uninjured. He dropped out, but McCluskey kept going.

In the Fletcher pits the crew expressed its rage. One mechanic hurled a wrench at the ground in angry frustration. "That no good McCluskey!" he complained when Jimmy returned to the pits.

Jimmy shook his head as though to indicate he bore Roger no ill will. "We were just racing," he said.

Later, handling problems forced Roger McCluskey to the sidelines. When Jimmy was walking through the pits soon afterwards, he met Roger coming the other way. McCluskey paused as though ready to say something when Jimmy, straight-faced, reached in the pocket of his uniform and produced a standard business card on which there was a printed message. Jimmy had been carrying that card with him for several months, awaiting the proper moment to produce it. He now handed the card to Roger.

The message read: *Ya' dumb shit!*

Jimmy smiled, winked at Roger, and walked away.

Jimmy had good times working for Bob Fletcher. At Trenton in April Fletcher Racing had two rental cars, one for Bob Fletcher's use, the other for Jimmy Caruthers'. Leaving the track after practice one afternoon, the two raced back to the motel, reaching speeds above eighty miles per hour down a four-lane highway, Caruthers on the inside, Fletcher on the outside. When they came to the motel entrance, Caruthers stomped on the brakes and skidded into the driveway. Fletcher braked at the same time and skidded into the motel parking lot almost door-to-door with his driver. Jimmy got out of his car, laughing: "Boss, you're a pretty good racer."

Jimmy placed fourth in the race at Trenton. But he had problems working for Bob Fletcher, many of them resulting from his own life-style, which clashed with that of the conservative Phoenix businessman who owned his car. A major problem was Jimmy's relationship with Suzie Grim. The fact that he and Suzie lived together openly, without benefit of a marriage contract, reportedly disturbed Bob Fletcher's wife, although she never criticized their relationship openly.

The Fletchers hosted a party at their home after the championship car race in Phoenix. Most of the guests arrived well dressed—although Arizona "well dressed" tends to be more casual than Eastern standards. Nevertheless, Bob and his wife were shocked to see Jimmy arrive, with Suzie, wearing Levi's and a T-shirt. Jimmy and Suzie brought with them a bottle of wine and sat down on the living room floor to drink from it.

In auto racing one of the main forms of pop art, next to the race cars themselves, is race jackets—shiny nylon, brightly colored, well adorned with patches and names. In keeping with well established tradition, the Fletcher Racing Team issued jackets to all members of its crew. The jackets were copper with turquoise trim, the official team colors, the same as on the race cars. "Fletcher Racing" was lettered on the back of each jacket, and the name of the person owning it was stitched on front. Jimmy received a jacket, as did others on the team, drivers and crewmen.

Jackets were also presented to the wives of most team members. Jim McGee's wife, Monty, received a jacket as did Jeannie Falk, wife of mechanic Ron Falk. No jacket, however, was offered to Suzie Grim. "They said they were really sorry," Monty McGee explained to her, "but they didn't want to give a jacket to a driver's girl friend."

When Jimmy learned of this slight to Suzie, he became angry. Suzie feared he might say something to Bob Fletcher that would jeopardize his ride and cautioned him, "I don't need a racing jacket."

"You *do*," insisted Jimmy, "but you don't need one of theirs!" He ordered a suede jacket custom-made in copper and turquoise, the colors of Fletcher Racing. The jacket cost more than a hundred dollars, ten times the cost of the nylon team jackets. Later, when Suzie wore it to the track, Jimmy told her how much better she looked than the wives of other team members. "Those other jackets are tacky-looking anyway," he claimed.

There was no sense of joy at Indianapolis in 1974. The dark clouds that rained on the 500 the year before still lingered over the Speedway. People remembered Art Pollard. They remembered Swede Savage. They remembered Armando Toran. They rarely talked about them, but they remembered. The sense of joy usually present in Gasoline Alley was gone. The practical jokers did not play practical jokes. Nobody wanted to hang around and talk. They came, did their work, and when they were finished, they padlocked their garage doors and left.

John McDaniels, team manager for Fletcher Racing, asked Suzie if she would like to score the race. This meant she would sit in the pits, keeping count of Jimmy's laps and recording his lap times on a score sheet. Suzie wanted to do it, but Jimmy refused to allow her. "It's too dangerous down in the pits," he snapped.

"Too dangerous?" she responded. "What about the danger for you?"

"I'm not worried about myself; I'm worried about you. That's who! Suppose I had an accident coming into the pits to refuel and the fuel tank caught fire. It's bad enough to be in an accident and hurt somebody you don't know. I never could live with myself if I hurt you."

Jimmy qualified easily for the 500 on pole day, earning a starting position in the fourth row. Gearbox problems forced him out of the race after only sixty-four laps.

He had done no drinking during the month of May, but that night, after the 500, he went out and got drunk, not falling-down drunk, but drunk. He rode his motorcycle to a party, Suzie on the back. Leaving the party, they decided it would be better for her to ride home with someone else. Jimmy did not like Suzie riding on his motorcycle when he was drinking, even only one beer, because two on a motorcycle made balancing difficult. Suzie rode home in a car with Jim and Monty McGee. Bob Fletcher's wife noticed and expressed her displeasure to others.

Mrs. Fletcher's comments eventually drifted back to Jimmy, infuriating him. "I'm not going to change my way of living to keep a ride," he told Suzie. "If that's what it takes to drive for Bob Fletcher, I won't drive for him!"

Suzie attempted to calm Jimmy, but he continued to express his anger: "Women should have no say in racing!" Jimmy insisted the place of women in racing was to give moral support to the drivers and the mechanics. Otherwise, they should stay the hell out of the way. "It's a business! A businessman doesn't call home and ask his wife if he should buy a certain stock."

Later Jimmy and Bob Fletcher openly argued. Jimmy was mad about his car breaking down. Bob, in turn, told Jimmy he disliked his motorcycle riding.

"Look," Jimmy responded. "Do you want a race driver or do you want a son?"

"I want a race driver," Bob snapped at him. "But I want one who won't break his back on some fool motorcycle and not be able to drive my race car."

But there were other, better days. One of them was at the Pocono 500 in July. With several laps to go, Jimmy ran third behind Roger McCluskey and A. J. Foyt. Suzie was worried. With fuel consumption designed both to emphasize better mileage and avoid a repetition of Salt Walther's fiery crash, each crew had less fuel in both the cars and in the pits. Jimmy's fuel consumption was high, and Suzie feared he might run out. On the last pit stop his crew drained practically the last drop from the refueling hoses into his car.

Suzie had a seat in the stands above his pits. She was so nervous that she began jumping up and down. Finally, one of Jimmy's crewmen motioned for her to come down, so she jumped the fence and joined them in the pits.

But it was Roger McCluskey, not Jimmy, who ran out of fuel with the finish line almost in sight. A. J. Foyt won the race, his first victory in a 500-mile event since the 1967 Indy 500. Jimmy placed second, his best finish in a championship car. Afterwards he told Suzie, "This is the happiest day in my racing career."

Toward the end of the summer Jimmy began to suffer pains in his back. At first he thought the pains were possibly the aftermath of one of his accidents in a race car. He had been banged around many times and might have pinched a nerve or damaged some muscle, or so he speculated. He also knew his father had arthritis, so questioned Doug about that ailment: "What does arthritis feel like?"

"Hurts like hell," said Doug.

"Maybe that's my problem."

With the Midwest racing season ended, he headed west once again, stopping in Idaho to visit his grandfather. Suzie remained in Indianapolis at her job, but made plans to join him on the coast at the end of November. Jimmy settled into the La Palma apartment he shared during the winter with Gene Romero. The night after arriving he dined with his mother and mentioned the back pains. La Vey Caruthers decided her son's back must really be bothering him. It was unusual for Jimmy to complain about anything.

"Maybe you should see a doctor," she advised.

"If the pain gets any worse, I will," her son protested.

Back in the apartment he discovered that hot baths seemed to relieve the pain. Burritto noticed his roomate began to spend more and more time soaking in the tub.

One day in mid-November Jimmy visited the shop

where Don Edmunds built midget race cars. Jimmy leaned against a frame and said little, letting Edmunds do most of the talking. Edmunds decided his friend did not look good. "What the hell's the matter with you, Caruthers?" asked Edmunds. "Got the flu?"

"I don't know," Jimmy replied, "but I sure as hell don't feel good."

"Don't worry," Edmunds encouraged him. "It's probably only cancer."

Jimmy grinned wryly. He told the car builder about the back pains that bothered him for several months. Recently his stomach also began to act up. "I fell off my bike last month and the handlebar hit me in the gut. That's probably it."

"Yeah," said Edmunds. "That's probably it. Guys like you shouldn't get on a motorcycle unless it has training wheels."

"Thanks," said Jimmy, turning to go.

"Don't mention it," said Edmunds, laughing, and he returned to his work. He thought his friend looked subdued. He later said to one of the mechanics in the shop, "That's not the usual Jimmy."

Although few people then realized it, Jimmy learned several months before that his father had cancer. Doug had been having trouble urinating, and his wife, Dana, kept telling him to go to the doctor. She figured he had some form of kidney problem. Ever stubborn, Doug kept refusing until it became too painful, but finally saw a urologist, who told him he had cancer of the prostate gland.

Fortunately the cancer was not too far advanced. The urologist merely gave Doug some medication, female hormones, to shrink the gland, planning surgery several months later. It did worry Jimmy, however, and drew him closer to his father than at any time since his brother's death.

Jimmy and his father were alike in that neither one of

them seemed able to show love and affection for each other. Their communications, in this respect, were minimal. Doug would tell Dana something, and she would tell Suzie, and Suzie would tell Jimmy. Then Jimmy would say something to Suzie, who would pass it on to Dana, and she would tell Doug. It was not that Jimmy failed to love his father; he just failed to show it. But after he learned Doug had cancer, Jimmy started coming by the shop more often. He dropped by for a couple of minutes every day—something which he had not done before. There was a new tenderness in the way he treated his father.

At the final championship car race of the season in November in Phoenix, Jimmy finished in eighth place, a half dozen laps behind the winner. He completed the year fifth in the USAC championship car point standings with 2,065 points and $95,023 in prizes. Since he also drove midget and dirt cars, his gross earnings for 1974 came to $101,019.

Bob Fletcher, however, was not pleased. By any normal standard, his two-year-old team had achieved tremendous success, particularly since his young driver had been forced to work with four different chief mechanics during that relatively short period. Yet Fletcher was rankled that he still had not been rewarded with a single victory. He also felt the pinch financially. One of the team's major sponsors, the Firestone Tire Company, decided to drop out of the sport because of their unwillingness to match Goodyear's investment.

After the Phoenix race he called the team together and admitted, "I may not be in racing next season." He wanted them to know in advance so they could protect themselves should he not field a team. Several members of the team soon obtained other positions. Jim McGee joined Roger Penske's race team based near Philadelphia. Ron Falk went to work for STP Products in Santa Monica.

Jimmy Caruthers had one more year remaining on his original three-year contract with Bob Fletcher, but the contract remained valid only as long as Fletcher went racing. The father-son relationship between Bob and Jimmy had soured. Bob disliked Jimmy's drinking, his smoking, his motorcycle riding, and his entire life-style, which included living with a girl. Bob might have tolerated this had Jimmy won races, but Jimmy did not win races. He began to wonder whether or not he chose wisely in building his team around a young driver. Bob Fletcher felt he was paying for Jimmy's inexperience. At the same time Jimmy was paying for Fletcher's inexperience.

Nevertheless, Fletcher did not completely disband the team after Phoenix, and he did not, as some people later suspected, fire Jimmy Caruthers. Jimmy returned to Anaheim aware that he might have a ride with Fletcher in 1975 or he might not. It was a troubled time for him, but not entirely untypical for those in his profession. Drivers often spend nervous winters negotiating rides for the spring.

On Wednesday before Thanksgiving Suzie arrived from Indianapolis on a short vacation from her job. She and Jimmy had been planning a trip to Mexico after the racing season for nearly six months. They wanted to go camping in San Felipe, a small Mexican town on the upper Baja peninsula, overlooking the Gulf of California. They talked up the trip so long and so enthusiastically that soon a small army of race people agreed to go, although in separate groups. Gene Romero planned to travel with them, as did Doug and Dana. Jim McGee and several others had already started for San Felipe, but Jimmy wanted to drive in the Grand Prix race at Ascot Park before leaving. He still had hopes of winning on Turkey Night.

Victory would be denied him again, however. Midway through the feature event, as Jimmy approached the first turn, two cars spun in front of him. Unable to stop, he collided with one. Other cars, approaching from behind, could not stop in time either. One struck Jimmy's car sideways and catapulted over him, ripping his windshield off and striking Jimmy a glancing blow on the shoulder. As the dust settled, Jimmy unbuckled his safety harness and stepped out of the severely damaged car. He seemed uninjured, but began stretching his arm where the car had brushed him.

Doug inquired, "You hurt?"

"Nothing broken," Jimmy replied.

After the race they left immediately for Mexico. Jimmy drove his pickup truck with a trailer for their motorcycles. Gene Romero drove a motor home rented from a friend who owned a gas station. They stopped in a Denny's restaurant near San Diego and breakfasted with Pancho Carter and his group, also headed for Mexico. They drove all night and in the early morning arrived at the campsite on the north side of San Felipe chosen by McGee.

"There's no place here to go riding," Jimmy complained. So their caravan continued to the south side of town, picking another campsite overlooking the Gulf of California. It had no running water, but there was plenty of open land. Soon Jimmy, Burrito, and Doug climbed on their motorcycles and went speeding down the beach, skidding in the wet sand, roaring up over the hills and into the barren countryside.

Jimmy rode his father over the roughest terrain he could find. The three men baited each other, daring the other to do some impossible trick, hoping he would fall on his face so they could all laugh. Doug returned, sand in his shoes, sand in his nose, sand coming out of his ears—but he loved it.

On their second day at San Felipe Jimmy decided it was time Suzie learned to ride a motorcycle. "I want you to ride very slowly," he instructed, measuring every word, "right where I can watch you."

"You make me nervous," said Suzie. She seemed bothered.

"Why do I make you nervous?"

"If I miss a shift, you'll probably get all upset."

"I don't care if you miss a shift," snapped Jimmy, beginning to get irritated. "I just don't want you breaking your fool neck."

"Look who's worrying about whose fool neck," said Suzie, knowing she had the upper hand now.

"Me!" shouted Jimmy. "I worry. Your mom made me promise to take care of you."

"I don't worry when you drive at Indianapolis," she teased him in a sing song voice.

"You don't have any compassion. Besides, you said you took two Valiums each time I drive there."

Burritto gave lessons to Nancy, who rode awkwardly off on her motorcycle, slid while turning on loose ground, and landed face down in the sand. Jimmy and Gene thought that funny. While they helped Nancy up, Suzie disappeared over a hill.

"Now where did she go?" mumbled Jimmy. "You can't trust women."

Ten minutes later Suzie reappeared, walking on the same hill she had gone over.

"Where's your bike?" Jimmy asked.

Suzie began to cry.

"Did you have an accident?"

"No."

"Then how come your arm is bleeding?"

"I ran into a barbed wire fence."

"Oh, that's beautiful," said Jimmy having a hard time trying to suppress a laugh.

Suzie saw this and became angry. "I knew you'd say that. Did I complain when you broke your ankle at Pocono?"

"I didn't run into a barbed wire fence at Pocono. Let me see the arm."

"Ouch."

"God, that makes me sick," he groaned.

"*You* make me sick," she huffed.

They washed Suzie's wounds, Jimmy warning her that she probably would come down with tetanus. Later they cooked hamburgers. They had forgotten to bring a grill, so they built a fire beneath the metal loading ramp on the rear of the motorcycle trailer. Suzie remembered them as the best hamburgers she had ever eaten.

All six slept in the motor home, Jimmy and Suzie in the compartment above the driver's seat. In the middle of the night Suzie awoke, bothered by Jimmy's tossing and turning. "My back is killing me," he admitted.

"I thought you told me it was feeling better."

"Must have been that crash at Ascot. I could have tweaked something again."

They got up and walked on the beach. The sky was clear, the stars above sharp pinpoints of light. The only sounds came from the gentle brushing of the waves upon the shore. For a long time they walked in silence, hand in hand, Jimmy breaking stride occasionally to kick at a rock. "When you get back, you're going to see a doctor," Suzie commanded.

"Yeah."

"You promise?"

"I promise."

The next day they drove to the other campsite north of San Felipe and joined McGee and the others. Jimmy brought his Jet Ski with him and rode it in the gulf. Later they learned that the area was infested with sharks.

"We could have gotten killed," worried Burritto.

"Not you," Jimmy insisted. "Any self-respecting shark would spit you out."

"I'm not worried about being swallowed by a shark," Burritto countered. "It's the *tasting* that scares the hell out of me."

After Suzie flew back to Indianapolis, Jimmy called Dr. Michael F. Callaghan, the orthopedist who presided over his miraculous return to racing following his Pocono injury. Jimmy had maintained a loose contact with Dr. Callaghan in the two intervening years, telephoning him occasionally. He called one December to wish him a merry Christmas. After Salt Walther's first lap accident at Indianapolis in 1973, Jimmy called to inquire if Dr. Callaghan would participate in Walther's rehabilitation. Dr. Callaghan suggested he knew only about bones, not burns, and that better qualified physicians in the Midwest might prove more suitable.

That same summer Dr. Callaghan became an accident victim himself when a woman rammed his car on the freeway. He suffered severe lacerations on his skull and arm. While in the hospital rcovering from those injuries, he received a telephone call. "Hey, Doc," the person on the line complained. "I don't try to operate on people. Why the hell are you stealing my thunder crashing your damn automobile?"

"Who is this?" asked Dr. Callaghan.

It was Jimmy Caruthers.

So when his back continued to bother him, Jimmy finally went to his trusted, old friend, Dr. Callaghan, figuring that if he could screw his broken ankle back together almost overnight, a minor problem like a sore back would be no sweat.

"Say the magic words, Doc," said Jimmy when he appeared at Tustin Community Hospital for his first appointment with Dr. Callaghan in early December.

"What words?" asked the orthopedist.

"The magic mumbo jumbo you used to cure my ankle. My back is killing me."

Dr. Callaghan smiled and began asking questions about the possible cause of the back pain. Jimmy explained he flipped his midget in a race toward the end of the summer. Then there was the Turkey Night accident, although the back pain began before then. On another occasion he had been jumping his motorcycle Evel Knievel-style off a ramp and fell, the handlebars digging into his stomach.

"Did the back pain start after then?"

"I'm not certain."

"You might have pulled a muscle in your back, then or almost anytime. These various accidents you describe may have merely aggravated the injury and caused it to get worse." Dr. Callaghan began to probe the muscles of Jimmy's back with his fingers. Jimmy had difficulty helping Dr. Callaghan pinpoint the source of the pain.

"All I know is my back is killing me," repeated Jimmy. Sometimes the pain gets so bad I have to sit up at night."

Dr. Callaghan frowned. "Does sitting up make your back feel better?"

"It helps," admitted Jimmy, "but I sure don't want to spend the rest of my life sleeping in a chair."

"Certainly not," said Dr. Callaghan. At the end of the examination Dr. Callaghan recommended that Jimmy report to Paul Pursell, the hospital's physical therapist, who had helped rehabilitate his ankle. He also ordered X-rays to determine whether the various accidents might have caused some bone damage. He said he did not expect to find any, but, "It's a precaution we don't want to overlook."

After Jimmy left and the nurse came in to retrieve Jimmy's records, Dr. Callaghan looked up at her. "I'm a bit worried about Jimmy," said the doctor.

The nurse paused. "Complications?"

"I'm not sure yet," Dr. Callaghan continued. "Jimmy says he can't sleep at night unless he sits up in a chair. That sounds a bit ominous. At least, it doesn't sound like the symptom for a pulled back muscle."

"Do you think it might be something worse?"

Dr. Callaghan paused and thought for a moment. "Well,

let's put it this way. It is as though a patient who had not been dieting came into my office and said he lost sixty pounds."

When he reported to the hospital X-ray office, the nurse behind the desk looked at Jimmy and smiled. "You mean to tell me race drivers get sick?" she asked.

Jimmy looked at her, puzzled. He did not recall meeting that particular nurse on any of his previous visits to the hospital. "I'm not exactly sick," he explained. "I have a back ache."

"I'm Shirley Fitzpatrick."

Jimmy smiled. He still was not certain he knew her.

"I'm Jack Fitzpatrick's wife," the nurse added.

"Oh hell, yes," said Jimmy. "I didn't know you worked here."

Jimmy had never met Shirley Fitzpatrick before, but he knew her husband, Jack. He was the owner of the race car in which his brother, Danny, had died. Ironically, a year later another driver died driving the same race car, so Fitzpatrick had since sold it.

As they talked Jimmy learned that Shirley Fitzpatrick grew up in a racing family. Her father was Foster Campbell, who sponsored a midget on the USAC circuit at the time Jimmy first raced in the Midwest. Her brother, Bobby Campbell, lived in Colorado. In 1970, when the USAC tour visited the Rocky Mountain area, he assisted Jimmy as a pit crewman.

Although she saw Jimmy race numerous times, they had never been formally introduced. In 1969 Shirley visited the Houston Astrodome for an indoor midget race. Before qualifying, Jimmy cruised up and down the fence on his motorcycle, assessing the crowd. He stopped and tried to pick Shirley up, but she politely brushed him off. Her father was standing only ten yards away. When they met at the hospital, however, she did not mention the encounter to Jimmy.

The following day, when Jimmy called Dr. Callaghan's office for a report on the X-rays, the nurse said the orthopedist wanted to speak to him. "I'm afraid it's nothing quite so simple as a broken bone," admitted Dr. Callaghan.

"Then what is it?"

"I don't know, but I can't help you." Dr. Callaghan recommended the name of another physician who also practiced at Tustin Community Hospital. He had offices across the street in a small office building on Newport Avenue. His name was Dr. Philip Hauser. "He's a good man," recommended Dr. Callaghan. "Young guy. Very enthusiastic. Good reputation in the hospital. The kind all the nurses go to when something's bothering them."

"You're not sending me to an obstetrician, are you Doc?" laughed Jimmy. "Because that's not what's bothering me."

"No, he's a surgeon. But he'll do a better job finding out what's wrong with you than a bone doctor like myself."

"Would you go to him?"

"Yep."

"Then that's good enough for me."

When Jimmy reported to Dr. Hauser's office several days later, he was told to strip and lay down on the examining table. Dr. Hauser asked him to breathe deeply and pressed down on his stomach. "You've been complaining of abdominal pain in addition to the back ache?" asked the physician. Jimmy admitted that to be true.

Dr. Hauser moved to a lighted glass board on which were attached the X-rays taken of Jimmy's stomach. "Well, we know something's in there, but we don't know what."

"Maybe I swallowed a beer can."

The physician failed to smile. "Probably nothing you swallowed. It could be that you suffered some sort of internal injury when you fell off that motorcycle. Maybe some vascular damage in the blood vessels around your aorta." Dr. Hauser suggested to Jimmy that they continue with additional tests to determine the nature of the injury. "It might be easier if you checked into the hospital."

Jimmy seemed startled. "In the hospital?"

"Yes," said Dr. Hauser quietly. His face was expressionless, giving no hint as to what was on his mind.

"You think it's that serious?"

"I don't necessarily believe it's serious," the doctor corrected him, speaking evenly. "I just can't tell at this point the cause of your discomfort. We need more tests, and those tests are best done here. If we can't find out what's wrong, we may have to do exploratory surgery."

Jimmy winced. "Surgery?"

"I'm not prescribing that now. We may discover the answer before that becomes necessary."

Jimmy sat silently for a moment. He was thinking. As a race driver he was accustomed to being hurt, so that part did not bother him. What bothered him was the possibility of missing races.

"Is this going to interfere with my driving?" asked Jimmy.

"When is your next race?"

"February."

"Then you're better off getting whatever needs to be done over with now. If the pain continues, it probably *will* affect your driving."

Jimmy nodded, conceding that the doctor had a point. "Okay," he said finally. "Let's do what has to be done."

That night Jimmy called Suzie long distance. "Good news," he announced, trying to sound cheerful.

"Your back is better?" she asked, hopefully.

"I've decided to check into the hospital and get it fixed." Her face froze.

"You call going into the hospital good news?"

"I figure there's no sense playing around any longer." Jimmy talked rapidly, as though trying to convince himself. "Get in and get it over with like I did with my broken ankle. The same doctors are working on the case. They'll fix me up real fast, and I'll be ready to go racing again."

"What's the problem?" probed Suzie. She sounded more worried than he.

"They figure I pulled something, but don't know what. They want to run some more tests. Then they'll probably give me two aspirins and send me home to bed with a whopping big bill."

"Do you want me to come out there?" she asked slowly, hoping he would say yes.

"Are you kidding? You were just here last week. Don't you like your job?"

"I'm just worried about you."

"Well, I'm worried about our bank account," said Jimmy sternly. "Aspirin costs money. Look, I'll be in and out of the hospital faster than a pit stop at Indy. When I come east for the USAC banquet, we can celebrate a late Christmas together."

"I love you, Jimmy."

"I love you, too."

After she hung up the receiver, Suzie sat by the telephone, nervously drumming her fingers on the table. She wondered if Jimmy was telling her the entire truth. But she could hardly complain. She was the one who nagged him to do something about it. For a while she debated with herself whether to pack a suitcase and climb on the next airplane to California to be with him. But maybe it was just tests. He would get mad at her for spending their money on a foolish trip. She decided to stay in Indianapolis and wait, but felt uncomfortable doing so.

On Tuesday, December 17, 1974, Jimmy Caruthers checked into Tustin Community Hospital. Kay Smith, the assistant head nurse in Surgery 100, looked at his admissions jacket. She thought the name Douglas James Caruthers, Jr., sounded familiar. "Who's this?" she asked one of the other nurses.

"Don't you know Jimmy Caruthers?"

"No. Who is he? Some football player?"

"He's an automobile driver. He races at Indianapolis."

"Oh," said Kay Smith. "I never follow racing."

Jimmy spent the next several days being felt and probed, swallowing nasty-tasting liquids, submitting himself to scrutiny by various machines, walking in his robe and pajamas from one section of the hospital to another, but most of the time waiting. He watched television, slept, talked to the nurses, had dinner, slept some more. He began to get bored, anxious. To relieve his nervousness he telephoned friends, sometimes talking to them for long periods of time without bothering to mention where he was.

He talked to Bob Fletcher, and people around Bob Fletcher, to see if he could catch some hint as to the owner's plans for the coming racing season. Fletcher seemed noncommital and the people around him had no idea what the car owner planned. Jimmy worried that Fletcher might be considering a new driver for 1975. He had a contract for one more year, but wondered if the Phoenix businessman would honor it. He talked to other owners, and people around other owners, and suggested that he might be available for 1975 if the right arrangements could be made. He asked that they get back to him, but did not give them the number of the hospital.

He talked to Gene Romero: "If anyone calls, tell them I'm away for a few hours. Don't tell them where I'm at."

"I understand," said Burritto.

When Suzie called, she asked, "Any news?"

"Only that I get handsomer every day."

"That's not news. You just tell those pretty nurses to stay away from you, or I *am* flying out."

After several days of testing, Dr. Hauser appeared in Jimmy's room one afternoon and sat down. "We're narrowing it down," he quietly explained, "but we still don't have the complete answer."

"What do you have?" Jimmy inquired, trying hard to conceal his nervousness.

"There's some sort of obstruction."

"An obstruction?"

"It could be one of three things," said the surgeon, and began ticking them off on his fingers. "First, it could be an aneurysm."

"What's that?" Jimmy looked puzzled.

"It's an enlargement of the wall of the artery. It could have been caused by an injury, getting bumped in a race car."

"And if it's not that?"

"Second, it might be a tumor, a swelling of some sort. A mass of new tissue that has no physiological function."

Jimmy seemed startled by this last explanation.

"I'm not saying you have a tumor," Dr. Hauser quickly added. "I'm just listing it as one of three possibilities."

Jimmy now was worried. "And the third?"

"A leakage of the aorta. That's the main artery leading into the heart. Again, this might be related to some past accident that seemed unimportant at the time. So we're going in to take a look around."

"The knife?" asked Jimmy. He looked uncomfortable as he said it.

"Exploratory surgery," Dr. Hauser continued. "Because of the position of this obstruction, there is no way to determine its nature without surgery. I'll conduct the operation and will have a vascular surgeon standing by. If the damage is, indeed, vascular, he will take over and make the repairs."

Jimmy reached behind his neck with one hand and began rubbing it nervously. "I guess there's not much choice."

Dr. Hauser began writing in the chart on his lap. He said

nothing while scribbling a series of instructions concerning preparations for the operation. Finished writing, he snapped the chart shut and stood up. "I've scheduled surgery for tomorrow morning. I'll see you then." The surgeon walked out of the room and headed down the hall to his next patient.

Jimmy reached for the telephone to call Suzie and tell her about the latest developments, then thought better of the idea. No sense alarming her. She was just worried enough to hop on the next plane and come out here.

That evening Jimmy's mother visited him in the hospital. As she left she told him, "I'll see you early in the morning."

"What for?"

"I want to see you before you're taken into surgery."

Jimmy smiled. "You don't watch me drive at Indianapolis. That's a much more dangerous place than this operating room. So why are you going to be here?"

His mother could not answer him.

8

Jimmy Caruthers felt the rush of wind past his helmet, the scream of the engine behind his back. His arms in front of him, hands gripping the steering wheel, jiggled as his car bounced over uneven spots in the pavement. He rotated his arms slightly left, and he could feel the pull of gravity pushing him to the opposite side of his seat as he swept through the third and fourth turns at Indianapolis.

He came off the turn, sliding almost up against the wall, then leveling off, feeling the buffeting of the air pushed aside by his racing machine bouncing off the wall back against him. The scream of the engine grew louder as its revolutions increased going down the long straightaway. He was traveling down a narrow tunnel formed by the thousands of fans packed in grandstands on both the left and the right.

He came past the entrance to the pits and the concrete wall behind which crouched crewmen flashing information on black slate boards. He glanced at his board, saw he was maintaining his same average speed, then looked up at the tower mid-straightaway, where the starter was waving a yellow flag, a signal to slow down. Jimmy rushed beneath the flag, then realized it was being waved not by the starter, but by Suzie Grim. Suzie waved the flag frantically at him.

He released his foot from the throttle, but the scream of the engine continued behind him, revving higher, higher, as though the throttle were stuck. In a panic he shoved down on the brake pedal to slow his advance, but the pedal pushed all the way to the floor. As he neared the end of the straightaway, the warning numbers flashed past him— three, two, one—and he twisted the steering wheel in his hands so as not to hit the wall straight on. Nothing happened. The steering wheel turned, but it felt loose in his hand. He was out of control. He continued rushing into the turn, faster, faster and faster.

Then suddenly he was past the turn and still going straight. The thousands of fans on both sides of him had disappeared, however, and there were nothing but walls with pictures of flowers and landscapes and ocean scenes hanging on them and a ceiling with fluorescent lights. He was in a long, long corridor at the end of which was a double door. Standing before the door was Suzie Grim, still waving the yellow flag, even more frantically than before.

Just as he was about to crash into the double doors, Suzie disappeared, and now he was reclining in the cockpit of his race car, looking up at his pit crew at Indy. A jack slid under the chassis, lifting him off the ground. The pit crew wore floppy green smocks with caps on their heads and masks across their faces, and they were changing the tires on his car, filling it with fuel, polishing his windshield. The crew chief had earphones and a headset mike and held a metal folder in one hand. He leaned toward Jimmy and shouted over the noise of the idling engine. "We've got bad news and good news," he said.

Jimmy realized the crew chief was Dr. Hauser. "What?" he asked.

"We have bad news and good news," repeated the surgeon.

"Tell me the good news first."

Dr. Hauser glanced down at his metal folder. "We can cure it," he announced.

"You can what?"

"We can cure it!" the surgeon shouted.

Jimmy was about to ask him what it was they planned to cure, but suddenly he jarred down off the jack. The pit crew pushed him back out through the double doors into the long corridor, then suddenly the walls disappeared and he was rushing down the straightaway at Indianapolis once more, crowds pressing him on both sides, flashing past the starter's tower again. Suzie Grim stood atop it, waving a white flag at him, indicating one lap to go. "One lap to go," thought Jimmy Caruthers. "If I can only get my car under control, I can win this race!"

He was back in his hospital room, trying to piece together what information he had. Dr. Hauser told him he had cancer. That was the bad news. Jimmy shifted uncomfortably in his hospital bed. The pain in his back remained, dulled by the local anesthetic which began to wear off. The good news. What was the good news? Dr. Hauser announced he had cancer, but said he thought he could cure it. Or was that part of the dream?

Jimmy glanced up and saw his mother sitting in a chair near his bed. He wondered how long she had been sitting there without his knowing it.

"Call Suzie," Jimmy told his mother. "I want her here."

Mrs. Caruthers did not respond immediately. "I'm sworn to secrecy, but—"

"But what?"

"She's already on the way."

147

"She's already on the way? I told her to stay in Indianapolis. Where is she now?"

"Las Vegas."

"Las Vegas? I'm dying of cancer, and she stops off in Las Vegas." He smiled for the first time since coming out of the operating room.

"The Los Angeles airport was fogged in," his mother explained, "so her plane landed in Las Vegas. She'll be here as soon as the weather clears."

It was afternoon by the time Dr. Hauser appeared again. Having shed his surgical gown, he now wore a white coat. He carried a metal record folder which he opened when he sat in the chair beside Jimmy's bed. Dr. Hauser began to speak, quickly but precisely, in words that seemed to duplicate those probably already written by him in the charts on his lap. "We explored your abdomen surgically and found a large tumor mass surrounding the aorta."

"The aorta?" asked Jimmy.

"The large artery that carries blood to the heart," the surgeon replied, then glanced down at the pages and continued, "The tumor extended superiorly to the stomach and the area of the small bowel and inferiorly down into the pelvis and to the kidney on either side. It's a pretty large mass. We took several biopsies of this mass—"

Dr. Hauser paused as though waiting for Jimmy to ask him to define biopsy. Jimmy did not, so Dr. Hauser explained anyway. "We actually cut some pieces of your tumor out to check them. The pathologist felt it was seminoma."

This time Jimmy did ask for an explanation.

"It's a form of cancerous growth," said the surgeon, "that develops in the testicular tissue. Some of them develop in the testicles themselves."

"The balls?"

"Right."

"You mean I've got cancer of the balls?"

Dr. Hauser smiled. "Not quite. It's merely *similar* to testicular tissue. What you have is a large growth in the stomach and near your heart, which is why we didn't dare remove it. But the samples we took indicate the tumor is pure seminoma, which does respond ninety percent to radiation. In fact, it's probably the most sensitive tissue to radiation therapy."

"So the odds are—"

"Good. Nine out of ten that we can shrink the cancer."

Jimmy stared ahead for several seconds. "Those are better odds than I have in a race car."

Dr. Hauser told him that one out of four people contract cancer at some point in their lives. Only one out of ten die of cancer. Many cancers are so slow-growing that the patient often dies of other "normal" causes—heart disease or cerebro-vascular strokes.

The surgeon outlined the treatment for the tumor—a series of radiation dosages over a period of sixteen weeks to shrink the tumor in his stomach. Dr. Hauser explained how he marked the tumor with metal clips so that the shrinkage might more readily be detectable on X-rays. "You mean I've got metal clips in my stomach?" asked Jimmy.

"Small metal clips," said Dr. Hauser. "They won't interfere with you in any way."

Jimmy affected a small chuckle: "Boy, I'm going to have fun getting on and off airplanes."

But something weighed on Jimmy's mind much more than the possibility that the metal clips in his stomach might trigger metal detectors in airports. There was a key question, now that the immediate threat of death from cancer had been dispatched from his mind, that weighed most heavily on his consciousness. "Will I be able to race?"

"If everything goes well," said Dr. Hauser, "you will be able to race."

"How soon?"

"How soon do you want to race?"

"The California 500 is in March. Indianapolis is in May."

Dr. Hauser consulted a calendar in his wallet. The radiation treatment would last twenty-one weeks, but there was a three-week rest period in the middle to permit the patient's resistance to recover. The surgeon estimated that he could schedule the rest period to occur at the time of the California 500. The treatment, assuming everything went well, should be finished in time for Jimmy to go to Indianapolis in May. "But I want to warn you," said the surgeon. "The treatments will make you weak. They'll make you sick, particularly at the start."

Jimmy did not seem to hear him. "As long as I can continue to race, I can live with what I've got," he said.

"Good."

"Besides, if Pops can take it, I can, too." Jimmy seemed to be speaking by rote.

"Your father has cancer?"

"Cancer of the prostate."

Dr. Hauser nodded. "If someone in your immediate family has cancer, it increases the odds that you will get it, too." He said it as though reading from a medical textbook.

"You mean it's hereditary? You catch it from your parents?"

Dr. Hauser frowned slightly. "That's probably putting it too strongly. But the same genetic factor present in the father may also be present in the son."

"What causes it?" asked Jimmy, now curious.

"Researchers are still asking that question. If I knew the answer, I could fly to Sweden and pick up a Nobel prize."

After Dr. Hauser left, Jimmy picked up the telephone and dialed his La Palma apartment. When Gene Romero answered, Jimmy told him, "Hey, partner, I've got cancer." He tried to sound cheerful as though cancer were some joke.

"I know," Burritto replied grimly. He had been at the hospital earlier, waiting with Jimmy's family.

"But they think they can shape it," Jimmy insisted. "As soon as they do, I'll be back out racing. It's just like a broken leg. As soon as it heals, you climb back in the car. Right?"

"Right!"

But Jimmy was not certain his roommate believed him. And Jimmy was not certain he believed himself. Mostly, he was not certain he believed Dr. Hauser. And did Dr. Hauser believe himself?

Did Dr. Hauser tell him the truth about his having a ninety percent hope of recovery? How do you figure odds in such a situation? Punch it up on a computer? "You have one chance in ten to recover. Thank you."

Does anybody recover from cancer—or do they just stall it? Is there a cure? Or is it just like battery acid, eating away your insides? Isn't cancer something like leprosy— because you have this dread disease growing inside you? Would people cross the street to avoid him? Would Suzie sleep with him? Can you transmit cancer to others like you transmit VD? I'm Jimmy Caruthers, the cancer patient. Don't cross me, or I'll piss cancer all over you!

Cancer. Big C! Whoever gave it that name anyhow? What was so big about cancer? It sounded like some cheerleader's cheer: *"Give me a C!"*

Jimmy Caruthers did not want to die, but he did not mind dying. Dying was something he accepted as one of the risks of his profession, almost a ritual of that profession. It came with the auto racing franchise. Dying was part of the sport, along with the fame and the money and the rent-a-car and the motels and the noise and the smoke and the girls hanging onto the fences outside the pits.

151

Getting snuffed was merely an occupational hazard. It was not worth giving much thought. If you minded getting snuffed, you did not race. It was that simple.

But dying of cancer? That was an insult—especially if it meant missing Indianapolis next year. If he had to die, let it be in a race car—like his brother, pitched against the roll bar. Or Art Pollard, upside down on the first turn at Indy. Or Jimmy Bryan, end over end at Langhorne.

Jimmy Caruthers did not relish the thought of dying in a hospital bed, growing progressively weaker, the flame dying from lack of fuel rather than being extinguished. He tried to put the thought of dying of cancer out of his mind, but failed, as he had failed to blot out the memory of Danny dying, and Art Pollard, and Jimmy Bryan.

Danger. Life is full of dangers. People call auto racing a dangerous profession, a brutal profession, a cruel profession, but auto racers racers do not die more often than normal people. They sometimes die sooner, but not more often. They sometimes die more dramatically, but not more often. They sometimes die in front of an audience of several hundred thousand spectators, some of whom may have paid precisely to witness their death. Everybody dies. Jimmy Caruthers would die sooner or later.

He did not object to that. He would just rather it be *later* than sooner.

He still had too many things in life to accomplish, such as winning Indy. He was on the right path and sooner or later it would happen—if he lasted long enough. If he lasted long enough to win Indy, would that make his life worthwhile? Was being the winner of the Indianapolis 500 enough? Was it merely winning Indy, or knowing you had won Indy, that made it all worthwhile? Was it climbing out of your car in victory lane and seeing your picture on the front page of newspapers all over the world the next day? Was it standing up at the awards banquet and having Tony

Hulman hand you a check for $250,000—sixty percent of which was not yours anyway? Would that make it worthwhile? Was it spending the rest of your life with people pointing at you, saying, "He won Indy," and having a million sports fans know your name because you once won Indy, and having that same name embossed on the glasses that Tony Hulman sends out for Christmas presents? Would all that make life worthwhile, or was it only the anticipation of all that?

And what about the other four billion people in the world who will not win Indy next year? How do they live with themselves, knowing they failed?

He must have dozed off because it was afternoon and he looked up to see Suzie standing in the doorway. He never saw her looking more beautiful before. She whispered, "A fine mess you've gotten us into, Caruthers."

He laughed at hearing a familiar line of hers. "Yeah, I guess I better be careful what toilet seats I use from now on."

She walked over and took his hand. She pressed it gently.

"How's Las Vegas?" he asked her.

"Never got out of the airport."

"Good thinking," said Jimmy, seemingly cheerful. "We're going to need all our money to pay these medical bills. I thought I told you to stay in Indianapolis."

"I thought I told you not to get cancer."

"Oh, yeah, I forgot," and made a face as though he had forgotten.

She sat down beside his bed, brushing her long hair back over her shoulders. For a long time neither of them spoke. Suzie looked at Jimmy, studying the features of his face, which she already knew so well. She wondered what their life together would be like from now on. Like Jimmy, she rarely thought much about their future beyond the next date on the USAC schedule. Theirs had been a day-to-day, week-to-week affair. Suddenly there was something in both their lives beyond the next race date.

Jimmy finally broke the silence. "Hey, are they telling the truth?"

"About the cancer? I'm afraid so." She was still joking.

He, however, was serious. "No, about being able to cure it."

"Yeah, I'm afraid so," she continued, joking.

"You wouldn't kid me, Babe?"

"No, it looks like I'm stuck with you, Caruthers," said Suzie still trying not to show the fear she felt.

"I was afraid they might not be giving me straight answers. Doctors don't exactly lie to you, but sometimes they don't tell all the truth."

"I spoke to Dr. Hauser," said Suzie, suddenly serious again. "He told me he thought he could cure it."

Jimmy seemed relieved by her comment. "That's what he told me."

Suzie said she saw no reason why Dr. Hauser would hide the truth from her. "If he told me you were dying of cancer, I guarantee I would tell you, too. I figure you're old enough to know."

"That's not bothering me," insisted Jimmy. "Is he telling the truth when he says I can go back to racing?"

For several days it seemed as though the telephone never stopped ringing. The sports reporters learned Jimmy had cancer, called, apologized, offered sympathy, then asked their questions. "That's right," Jimmy told them. "I woke up after surgery and thought I had had a bad dream. Then I found out it wasn't only a dream."

Race promoter J. C. Agajanian called. Aggie had an operation for cancer a year before and felt fine despite having a tumor removed from his chest. He was bothered only by shortness of breath if he moved around too fast. "I want to find out if you're getting the right treatment," Aggie stated. "How good's your doctor?"

"He's one of the finest specialists around," Jimmy told him.

"I want to make sure," said Aggie, "because my doctor is one of the best around, and I wanted to recommend him to you."

"Hey, no sweat, Aggie. We've got it covered."

Later, J. C. Agajanian spoke nearly two hours with Jimmy's mother to assure himself that her son was obtaining the best treatment available. Aggie was sold on his own physician and wanted Jimmy to see him, too. Aggie told Jimmy's mother he would even be willing to pay the bill. At the same time Aggie remembered that when he first came down with cancer, all his friends who had the disease before him wanted him to go to *their* physician, who reportedly was the finest. They even announced their willingness to pay the bill. Aggie finally decided not to pursue the matter any longer.

Bob Fletcher called from Phoenix and announced something that Jimmy did not know: his wife had had cancer for twenty years and had surgery five times as well as chemotherapy treatments. She was not supposed to live past her first operation, but somehow she confounded the doctors.

"Ma Fletcher did all that?" asked Jimmy. He was impressed.

"Jimmy," said Bob, "you've got some big odds against you, but they are a lot different from on the racetrack."

"That's true."

"Sometimes the odds get pretty slim out there."

Jimmy repeated to Fletcher the ninety percent odds quoted to him by Dr. Hauser and said he expected to be back racing again next year as soon as he completed his course of radiation treatments. Bob said nothing about whether there would be a Fletcher team racing in 1975.

Several days later, however, Jimmy read in the Los Angeles *Times* that Fletcher had completed his plans for the coming season, retaining Pancho Carter as one of his drivers. Billy Vukovich was being added to the team, presumably to take Jimmy's place. "It sounds like he's dropping you just because you've got cancer," said Suzie angrily.

"Bob wouldn't do that," Jimmy told her. "His wife has cancer. There are other reasons."

"You've got a contract with him. He can't fire you unless he wants to pay for the season."

"The money's not worth fighting over, Babe. I'll find a ride with someone else."

"It was sure nice of him to tell you when he called," Suzie snapped peevishly.

Jimmy smiled. "That's racing."

Shirley Fitzpatrick stopped by Jimmy's room one afternoon, taking a break from her job as X-ray technician. Suzie was visiting at the time and Jimmy introduced them: "See what fat nurses we have in this hospital." Jimmy pointed at Shirley's swelling stomach.

"She's not fat," Suzie explained. "Shirley's pregnant."

"I knew she was something."

"How soon are you expecting?" Suzie asked.

"Three months."

"She's going to name the baby after me," Jimmy suggested.

"I am not," Shirley protested. "If it's a boy, Jack and I plan to name the baby Ryan."

"Ryan! What kind of a name is that? You should name him after a race driver. If you won't name him after me, at least name him after A. J. Foyt, or Mario Andretti. But Ryan?"

Suzie turned to Jimmy. "Maybe we should have a kid," she suggested.

"Right here? In front of Shirley?"

But Suzie was serious. "If you go in for radiation treatments, maybe you'll become sterile, and we'll never have a chance again."

Jimmy laughed. "No way a big stud like me is going to let a little radiation get him down. Besides, Dr. Hauser promised me a lead jock." But Jimmy suddenly grew serious too. He turned to Shirley. "What's radiation like anyway? Does it hurt?"

Shirley Fitzpatrick thought it curious that a race driver like Jimmy Caruthers should be asking if it hurt.

Suzie and Jimmy spent Christmas eve together in the hospital. Before his illness, they decided they would not exchange presents during the holidays, but would celebrate Christmas in January when he returned to the Midwest for the indoor races in Fort Wayne. As a result, Suzie left his present—an expensive, hand-tooled leather briefcase with drawings of his championship car on one side and his midget on the other—back in Indianapolis. In order to have something to give him, she rushed out to a nearby shopping center and bought Jimmy a pair of boots. She expected nothing in return, but he surprised her with a gift of Indian jewelry purchased earlier in Hermosa Beach. He kept the jewelry locked in the hospital safe, and at the appropriate moment asked one of the nurses to bring it in.

"This jewelry is absolutely gorgeous," she screamed, and tried it on. Suzie kissed him. He grinned.

Suzie remembered it as a nice Christmas, not a sad one. She stayed until nearly midnight, then returned to the La Palma apartment. Several days later Jimmy came out of the hospital and Suzie flew to Indianapolis. She spoke to Bob Munro, president of Hoosier Solvents and Chemicals, for whom she worked as secretary. "Jimmy's going to be undergoing cobalt treatments all winter," she explained. "I think I'd like to be with him."

Munro said he understood. Suzie decided to return to California as soon as she could train a replacement. Fortunately, the woman who had held her job previously wanted to come back to work.

While Suzie was still in Indianapolis, Jimmy prepared for the radiation therapy. He already planned a return to racing. Normally a patient would wait several weeks after leaving the hospital before beginning treatment. (The treatment in Jimmy's case meant thirteen weeks of radiation spread out over sixteen weeks, with a three-week break in the middle.) But Jimmy wanted to drive Indy and already began to ask about possible rides, finding out which cars were available. One possibility was with Alex Morales, head of Alex Foods, a Southern California supermarket chain. Morales sponsored cars in local races and was thinking of going to Indy with Johnny Capels, his mechanic. "Don't hire a driver, Alex, until you check back with me," Jimmy told him. Morales promised to wait.

Dr. Hauser told Jimmy that in order to be ready for Indy in May, he would have to begin treatment immediately. He scheduled his first treatment with a radiologist in Fullerton for Monday, December 30. That morning Jimmy was starting to leave the apartment when Gene Romero told him, "I'm going with you."

"No," Jimmy replied. "I'm going this alone."

"Hey, we're going down there together."

"You don't need to go with me."

"No problem."

"Look, Burritto, the answer is no. I don't need a goddam nursemaid!"

"I don't want to hear it, Caruthers. You're not going to meet all those pretty nurses without me."

158

"In that case—" agreed Jimmy.

They drove to St. Jude's Hospital in Fullerton. After waiting a half hour in the reception room, the nurse told Jimmy and Burritto that the doctor would see them. They went into his office. The doctor studied a copy of Jimmy's records.

Jimmy appeared nervous. He looked at Burritto. Burritto looked back at him. Finally Jimmy asked, "Do you mind if we smoke?"

The cobalt treatment that day made Jimmy sick, but he tried to hide from his roommate how sick it made him. Several days later Burritto was out of town and Jimmy went to St. Jude's by himself. Afterwards he drove to Dr. Hauser's office for an examination. Dr. Hauser noticed that Jimmy appeared pale and exhausted. The nurse told him that Jimmy had vomited while waiting. "How are you feeling?" Dr. Hauser asked him.

"I'm feeling lousy," Jimmy admitted.

"Nauseated?"

"Yeah, really woozy."

"Who brought you here?"

"I drove myself."

Dr. Hauser became angry. After the examination he asked Jimmy for the keys to his car. Jimmy wanted to know why. "Because I'm driving you home, that's why," snapped the surgeon.

Dr. Hauser drove Jimmy to his mother's house. Jimmy attempted to joke about not being used to others driving him, but Dr. Hauser did not seem in the mood for humor. "You better rely on other people for help," he warned after they pulled up to the house in Anaheim. "Radiation treatment takes a lot out of you. You don't drive at the Speedway without people helping in your pits."

"I get your point," admitted Jimmy.

Later, Burritto came looking for Jimmy. He knocked on

his mother's front door, tried the back, and was ready to leave when Jimmy finally appeared at the door. "I felt pretty sick after the treatment," Jimmy admitted.

"You better stay here and let your mother take care of you," Burritto advised him.

"I can't. I don't have any clothes or shaving gear."

"I'll bring them to you." Burritto started to leave.

"Wait a minute," Jimmy called after him. "I'll go with you."

Burritto tried to argue Jimmy out of the idea, but realized that Jimmy wanted to do it himself. They returned to the La Palma apartment and threw some of Jimmy's clothes plus his shaving gear into a paper bag, then returned to his mother's. "You're going to stay here, where you can get some decent food and where somebody can watch you," Burritto insisted.

"Okay," said Jimmy. He thanked his friend for his trouble, then went inside to go to sleep and wait for his mother to come home. He stayed with her until Suzie returned from the Midwest.

No sooner had Suzie settled into the La Palma apartment, and the routine of daily treatments, than she received a telephone call from Indianapolis. It was Jimmy 's father. "Jimmy has to return for the USAC awards banquet," Doug insisted.

"Jimmy hates banquets," Suzie said, "and he's sick."

"I know," Doug replied, but explained that USAC planned to give Jimmy the award as most improved driver on the championship car circuit. The award was worth one thousand dollars. "It's supposed to be a surprise."

"Last year, when we lived in Indianapolis, he still didn't attend the banquet. He's not going to fly in from California feeling as bad as he does."

"You'll have to tell him about the award," decided Doug. "But don't tell anybody else."

Suzie informed Jimmy later that afternoon. She was right. He did not want to attend the banquet, even to accept a thousand-dollar check. "I suppose they could mail me the check," he mused. Finally, he decided to attend—not because of the money but because he feared his failure to appear would be considered a sign of weakness. The entire racing world, having heard of his cancer, would write him off as nearly dead. He did not want people feeling sorry for him, even from a distance of two thousand miles. "I want people to know I'm not going to let cancer lick me."

He flew to Indianapolis Saturday morning, January 18, stopping to change clothes at the house he and Suzie shared. Following the banquet, he returned to the house and discovered that burglars had forced open a window and ransacked the place, emptying drawers and jewelry boxes, scattering clothing all over the floor. "Just what I need," groaned Jimmy. "A burglary!"

He did not even have a telephone to call the police. That had been disconnected, so he went next door to use the neighbor's phone. As near as he could determine, the burglars did not take anything. There was not much to steal. Suzie had removed most of the appliances, bringing them to her family's home. The burglars apparently hit the house on a night when they expected its occupants to be attending the USAC banquet, not realizing the house stood vacant most of the previous month.

Jimmy sat up with the police until two A.M. He rose early the next morning to catch an eight A.M. flight back to California. When he arrived in Los Angeles, he felt exhausted.

He also felt the financial pressures caused by his illness. The year 1974 had been his most successful. He ranked sixth on the list of USAC money winners with $101,019. His share of that sum was $40,408. His contract with Fletcher also gave him $5000 for Indy, $2500 for Ontario, $1500 for Pocono, plus $1000 a month for expenses. He also earned some incidental money for appearances and endorsements, bringing his total income to nearly $70,000. He put a large percentage of this money, after taxes, in the bank.

In November, before learning he had cancer, Jimmy ordered a new automobile. He also made plans to buy an airplane, something he had always wanted. But with hospital bills mounting, he found his finances stretched. He accepted delivery of the car, but reluctantly postponed plans for the airplane.

His problem was lack of insurance. As a race driver, he had accident insurance through USAC, but never purchased health insurance on the assumption he would need medical care only because of a racing accident. He was wrong, and this miscalculation cost him dearly. He had to pay the entire $13,000 in medical bills out of savings.

Suzie knew they needed the extra money she could earn by returning to work, but she did not want to leave him. She planned to stay in California until the completion of his cobalt treatments. They sat up one night discussing her future. Suzie told Jimmy she found the nine-to-five office routine of a secretary's life too restrictive. "Maybe I'll get an airline stewardess job like Bev," she suggested.

"Hey, that would be neat," said Jimmy.

The next day they called a friend, Dave Gentry, an inflight supervisor for TWA. Dave promised nothing, but said he would ask if the airline was hiring stewardesses.

Jimmy and Suzie fell into a steady routine. Each morning at ten A.M. they reported to the outpatient clinic at St. Jude's Hospital, where he received radiation treatment from a linear accelerator. They sat in the waiting room along with the other patients who appeared regularly each day for similar treatment. These were people threatened with death, but Suzie noticed little fear in their faces, no more than if they were visiting a dentist to have a cavity filled. They waited fifteen minutes or so before the nurse called Jimmy's name. Then, while Suzie waited outside, he disappeared into the treatment room.

He often emerged from the treatment, as did the others, with small black X's marked on his face or parts of his body, indicating the area treated that day. Despite the outward calm he and the other patients displayed, Jimmy found radiation treatment a traumatic experience. The radiation caused him to lose all the hair from his body, even his pubic hair. He feared the hair on his head might also drop off, though it did not.

Sometimes Suzie talked to the others in the waiting room while awaiting Jimmy's reappearance. She got to know their faces and their ailments, but not their names. One man had had a kidney removed and was taking treatment from the linear accelerator to prevent cancer from spreading to the other kidney. He had a son who played high school football. He and Suzie talked about the son. An older lady had cancer of the uterus. Her radiation treatments were complete, and now she took chemotherapy—drugs which would hopefully arrest the spread of the cancer within her. Another man came with his wife. When she went in for treatment, he and Suzie talked.

For each one of them it was fifteen minutes out of their day. One patient arrived just before playing golf. A woman came in after shopping. One woman had skin cancer, and after each daily treatment she had X marks on her face. Her daughter brought her in a wheelchair. Suzie noticed there was hardly a sad face on any of them. If they experienced grief, they kept it well within themselves. They all seemed like nice people. They were a community of strangers brought together by coincidence, and they had a common interest—extending their lives.

The linear accelerator was a large X-ray device with interchangeable lenses that permitted the machine to be focused on different parts of a patient's body, or over the entire body. One week the radiation technician focused the accelerator on the area where the malignancy had been discovered. Another week the technician radiated Jimmy's neck, his bowels, his testicles. There was no pain involved, such as that caused by a dentist's drill, but whenever Jimmy lay down on the table and the machine dosed him with radiation, he felt as though his insides were boiling. He became nauseated, even while still on the table, and so nervous that he wanted to scream.

When the machine was shut off, he would rise from the table, feeling somewhat embarrassed at the panic he had felt and would reenter the waiting room looking little different from when he had left it fifteen minutes before. But he was exhausted and psychologically shattered. He took tranquilizers to curb his nervousness, other pills to cure his nausea, and still other pills to combat diarrhea.

Usually the two did not return immediately, but stopped at Don Edmunds' shop. On Edmunds' lunch break he and Jimmy raced radio-controlled race cars in the parking lot. Jimmy spent the noon hour racing these toy cars, then napped several hours. He awoke feeling refreshed and went on to other business, sometimes riding motorcycles with his son, Jimmy, who was three and a half years old. He recently bought little Jimmy a tiny Honda. But the tension remained.

Jimmy always had a sore throat. He began to release some of his pent-up emotions by snapping at Suzie, by complaining about petty matters. She did not retaliate because Dr. Hauser had warned that this would be Jimmy's reaction to the radiation.

Gene Romero was gone a lot of the time, readying his motorcycles for the coming season, so Jimmy and Suzie usually had the apartment to themselves. On weekends Burritto's girl friend, Nancy, sometimes came to stay. Burritto did not always get along well with Suzie, as though he and she were rivals for Jimmy's attention. But during this period they tried to stay out of each other's way.

One afternoon Suzie was sorting the laundry when a car owner called Jimmy. He needed somebody to test a sprint car at 605 Speedway. Jimmy grabbed his helmet and started to leave. Burritto and Nancy decided to accompany him. "Wait a minute," said Suzie. "I'm going, too."

"You can't go," Jimmy yelled at her. "You've got to do the laundry!"

So Jimmy, Burritto, and Nancy left for 605 Speedway, leaving Suzie crying in the apartment. Angry, she went to the hairdresser and had her hair done—and then she did the laundry.

Jimmy also became irritated if Suzie and Nancy talked too loudly and interfered with his concentration while watching television. He liked "M*A*S*H" and "Baretta," as well as sports events. "Stop that giggling," he would say.

"We're not giggling; we're just talking."

"If you girls have to talk, go in the bedroom."

Jimmy Caruthers was never an easy person to live with, as Suzie discovered during their more than three years together. Despite his reputation as a practical joker, he was an inward person who did not share his thoughts easily with others. He became even more difficult to live with during this period of treatment.

On several occasions when Jimmy snapped at her Suzie would flee to the bathroom, have a good cry, wipe her eyes, then return to the living room, pretending nothing had happened. She talked with Jimmy's father once about his moods: Why did Jimmy seem more irritable with her than with anyone else? "I don't know if it's me, or what," she said. "Am I bugging Jimmy too much?"

"No, you're the only one he can yell at," explained Doug. "That's the way it usually is with husbands and wives. You usually take it out on the one closest to you."

"But I'm not a wife," sighed Suzie. "I'm only a girl friend."

But there were other, more pleasant moments for Jimmy and Suzie during the winter of 1975. They spent a day touring Sea World. They drove down to San Diego to visit a store that distributed Jet Skis. They dined with Jimmy's mother and watched the Super Bowl on television. They went out with Don Edmunds and his wife. Another time they had dinner with Uncle Red and his wife, Jimmy's Aunt Virginia. They took Jimmy's young son to Disneyland and, on another occasion, to Knott's Berry Farm. They went to a motorcycle show with Burritto and Nancy.

Jimmy also spent time alone with his young son. Although he and Sally had been divorced, they remained friends. Sally never made it difficult for him to see young Jimmy. If Sally felt any resentment toward Suzie, she tried not to display it.

Jimmy's mother was "polite" to Suzie, but Mrs. Caruthers never thought of Jimmy's girl friend as another daughter, as she previously had thought of Sally. She merely tolerated Suzie Grim, who, after all, was not even married to her son.

She never said anything that openly embarrassed Jimmy's girl friend because it would embarrass Jimmy, too. She did not want to hurt him, but she resented Suzie having entered his life, perhaps being responsible for the dissolution of his marriage. If it wasn't Suzie that caused the divorce, then it was Jimmy's racing that caused the divorce, and Suzie was part of that.

Mrs. Caruthers disliked auto racing. It took the life of one son and she worried constantly that it might someday take the life of her second son.

But she kept her feelings buried inside her because she did not want to interfere with Jimmy's life. and she went on being polite in her relationship with Suzie Grim.

At regular intervals Jimmy returned to Tustin Community Hospital for X-rays to determine the progress of his treatment. Shirley Fitzpatrick often saw Jimmy and Suzie arrive together for an appointment. They sat together in the waiting room outside the X-ray department for hours at a time, reading magazines or just talking, waiting for the negatives to be developed. Shirley considered Suzie the perfect girl for Jimmy.

When not busy, Shirley frequently came into the waiting room and visited with them. Jimmy continued to kid her about being fat. By now Shirley was nearly nine months pregnant. One time he told Shirley, "Hey, Suzie's going to be a stewardess."

"Really?"

"Yeah. She's going to Kansas City for her final interview with TWA in another month. Pretty soon she'll be flying all over the country." Although Jimmy did not say so in so many words, Shirley sensed he was extremely proud of Suzie's future career.

Jimmy got along well with all the people at the hospital and at Dr. Hauser's office across the street. Regardless of what must have been going on in his mind, he displayed a contagious air of open cheerfulness. He found that others wanted to confide their secrets to him. Sue Rutton worked as a receptionist in Dr. Hauser's office. She talked to Jimmy and Suzie about having an operation herself recently. She and her husband had trouble conceiving a baby. "Gee, I could have helped you with that," Jimmy kidded her.

"You better not," Suzie warned him.

"Don't worry," the receptionist laughed. "I'm pregnant now."

When Dr. Hauser saw Jimmy, he examined the X-rays taken earlier that afternoon. "I think we're making progress," suggested the surgeon.

"That's the best news I've heard," smiled Jimmy. He

seemed relaxed. He no longer betrayed any fear of the unknown.

"The radiation treatment seems to be shrinking the tumor," said Dr. Hauser.

"How can you tell?"

"The clips we attached to it have moved closer together."

Jimmy looked at where the surgeon indicated on the X-ray films. There were several bright little dots. He could no more understand what the films showed that Dr. Hauser would understand the refinements on a Offenhauser engine. But he trusted his doctor as he had trusted Dr. Callaghan several years before. Dr. Callaghan had sped his return to racing, and Dr. Hauser would do the same.

"There's a midget race I want to drive in up in San Jose toward the end of February," said Jimmy.

Dr. Hauser nodded as though he already knew it. "It's time for the three-week break in your treatment schedule. There's no reason why you can't race."

"Thanks, Doc."

"But the purpose of the break is to allow you to regain your strength," cautioned the surgeon. "Don't overdo it."

Jimmy promised his doctor he would not, but the warning sailed over his head. He already was thinking about the preparations he must make to go to San Jose. His father was out of town, so he would need to do most of the work himself. He spent the rest of the week preparing his midget car for the race.

In previous years Jimmy always waited until the last possible minute to leave on the 400-mile trip north. He drove straight through in a big rush, raced, then straight home in another big rush, never straying from Interstate 5, the freeway that cut through California's San Joaquin Valley. This time he and Suzie decided to leave one day early, on Friday, traveling the longer but more scenic coastal route. Jerry Smith, a mechanic who worked in Doug's Anaheim shop, accompanied them, along with his girl friend.

They stopped during the day in San Luis Obispo at the Madonna Inn, a hotel with antique brass tables and chairs, and dolls decorating the rooms, for apple pie and ice cream. They halted the pickup while traveling along the cliffs near Big Sur to see the Pacific Ocean breakers pounding the beaches and rocks below them. "This is great," said Jimmy. "I should do this more often."

They arrived later in San Jose. The auto racing facility in that city contains a paved, third-of-a-mile high-banked track that drivers find very fatiguing to drive during long races. It particularly fatigues their muscles, and halfway through the race drivers can be seen with their heads laying over on their right shoulders, trying to sit straight up. That night's race was a hundred laps, and stamina would be a major factor.

In the early laps Jimmy battled Bobby Olivero for the lead. They raced almost side by side down the straightaway, bringing the fans to their feet to see who would give way as they slid into the turns. But two thirds of the way through the race Jimmy tired and slipped off the pace. Chuck Gurney eventually passed him. Jimmy finished third.

He had to be helped out of the cockpit after driving into the pits. He was exhausted. He complained of not having any strength in his arms. "I could race with him up until a point," he gasped, "but I couldn't hold on any longer."

That same night Jimmy made a comment to Gary Bettenhausen that was overheard and carried by the wire services to newspapers all over the country. It also appeared in *Sports Illustrated.* During one of the heat races Jimmy and Gary battled for the lead. Jimmy drove too hard into turn three and went sliding up the bank in front of Gary, almost hitting him. Gary hit the brakes and drove down beneath him, averting a wreck.

Afterwards Gary walked over to Jimmy's pits. "What

happened out there, Caruthers?" Gary asked. 'You're a wild man. You gave me a slide job that almost parked me outside the track."

Jimmy knew he had made a mistake, but offered no alibi; nor did he apologize. He began to chuckle. "Gary, don't ever try to outbrave a cancer patient!"

9

The following week practice began for the California 500 at the Ontario Motor Speedway. Reporters from the wire services, local newspapers, and magazines floated around the pits, looking for stories for their next editions. The television newsmen appeared, trailed by entourages of cameramen and technicians looking for stories for the evening news. The story they found was Jimmy Caruthers.

He no longer was Jimmy Caruthers, auto racer, usually friendly, easy to approach, always a good interview, but merely one of dozens on the championship trail. He was now Jimmy Caruthers, the man who had cancer, and as such was unique.

Whereas at most races the crowds of reporters and cameramen flocked to the pits of Bobby Unser, Mario Andretti, Johnny Rutherford, or the latest hot shoe, these crowds now found their way to Jimmy Caruthers. The reporters were polite and often began their interviews with innocuous lead-in questions—such as what did he think about his new ride with Alex Morales? But the question they wanted to ask, and Jimmy knew they wanted to ask, and sooner or later they *did* ask, was: What does it feel like to have cancer? The reporters had grown accustomed to interviewing men who faced death every time they stepped into a race car, but Jimmy Caruthers faced death in a different manner. It was a new angle, and reporters who previously needed to know only about turbochargers and pop-off valves and Offenhauser engines, now had to deal with terms like linear accelerators and seminoma.

Jimmy played their reporters' games and waited for the hidden question to be sprung at the end of the interview, just as he had the season after his brother, Danny, died. And everyone wanted to know: How can you continue racing with that hanging over your head?

"I still get tired quicker than I should," he told the reporters, "but other than that, I feel fine. The cancer is cured, but, hell, during the seven weeks I was taking radiation treatment I couldn't exercise, so I'm still a little on the weak side. I'm working on a race-to-race basis. I'll admit I didn't have much hope a couple of months ago, but I'm pretty optimistic right now. The doctors say I have it whipped, but they want me to return and have it checked now and then just to make sure it doesn't grow back. They think there's not too much chance it will. When I was lying there in the hospital, I just figured that if I really was going to die, it was okay because I think I've lived more at my age than a lot of people who live to be a hundred. Sure, I was scared of dying, but I didn't come apart at the seams! I'm working on a race-to-race basis, but I'm pretty optimistic now."

The reporters would thank him and walk off, still making notes in their notebooks, and Jimmy would climb back in his race car, or turn to find another reporter awaiting him with the same questions, or return to the parking lot outside the garage area where his Uncle Red parked a large mobile home so he could relax and get away from the questions and the stares of those who wondered if he was really cured. The headlines during the week chronicled his comeback: "Caruthers Now Facing New Foe Called Cancer," and "Cal 500 Not Caruthers' Biggest Race," and "Cancer Couldn't Brake Down Caruthers." Too bad you had to kill yourself, or come close to killing yourself, to get ink.

Even the other race drivers, usually the most irreverent lot of athletes in any sport, began to treat Jimmy Caruthers with a certain amount of deference. They were accustomed to members in their ranks horribly maimed, disfigured with burns and scars. They knew that many among them might die in a race car, but they were not certain how to deal with someone who had cancer, who had a tumor growing inside him. Race drivers are a superstitious lot, and they wondered if it had been something Jimmy did that caused him to get this cancer—his fast living, the exhaust fumes he breathed, some germ that still might be lurking around the speedways. They worried that if they got too close to him, they would catch cancer, too. And although they showed no outward concern over the continuous threat that a crash at a hundred eighty miles per hour posed to their own, and others', lives, they worried whether cancer might soon cause the loss of their friend. It was a chink in the racers' armor. They could deal with sudden death, but lingering death was something they would just as soon not witness.

Nevertheless, they stopped by Jimmy's pits, or his garage, or Uncle Red's mobile home to chat about automotive matters and talk racing, but sooner or later got around to the same question all the reporters were asking Jimmy. They wanted to know about his cancer, and after Jimmy told them he was cured, they sometimes cornered Doug or

Suzie afterwards. "Jimmy says he's cured," Indy 500 winner Johnny Rutherford asked Suzie one afternoon, "but how is he *really* feeling?"

So to ease the pressure Jimmy made a joke of it, together with Lee Kunzman, who appeared at Ontario to drive in his first race after his accident at the same track more than a year before. The drivers and reporters, after probing Jimmy's cancer, often went on to inquire about Lee's physical status, the long-range effects of the concussion and paralysis he suffered. So whenever Jimmy and Lee saw each other, they exchanged comments about their injuries.

"Hey, Caruthers, how's your cancer today?"

"Fine, Lee. How's your busted head?"

"It was still on when I shaved this morning, Caruthers, but I'm more concerned about your cancer. How is it— *really?*"

"It's really fine, Lee. *Really* fine!"

On March 2 both recuperated drivers competed in 100-mile qualifying heats for the California 500 the following weekend. Lee Kunzman placed third in the first one, and Jimmy Caruthers took fifth in the other one—which silenced the questioners for a while.

But while he tolerated the questions of reporters and other drivers at the track, and found time to joke about this, the underlying tension often overflowed once he got back to the apartment at night. Rather than stay at a motel near the track, he chose to commute back and forth to La Palma. One reason was to get away from everybody during the evening, but another important reason was financial. Unlike Jimmy's previous team, the Morales team was underfinanced and did not have extra money for lavish living at Holiday Inns. Jimmy remained so uncertain about how long the ride might last that he chose not to put the number 5 (earned by his fifth-place finish in the point standings in 1974) on the car. He raced with number 78 instead.

One evening he arrived home from the track and Suzie had dinner waiting on the table. "Why are we eating so early?" he barked at her. "Don't you know I need time to relax?"

The following night Jimmy arrived home from the track and discovered Suzie had not yet begun to prepare dinner. "How come dinner's not ready?" he complained.

He threw his helmet bag across the room and slumped down on the sofa. For more than a minute he stared at the floor, the realization growing upon him how impossible he had become to live with. Finally, he looked up at Suzie with a sad expression on his face.

She looked at him and realized he was sorry. "I know," she said, and came over and took his hand.

"I haven't been very easy to live with lately."

Suzie said nothing, and for several minutes they sat on the sofa hand in hand. Like him, she lived from day to day.

On Saturday Jimmy drove in the California 500. On the fifty-fourth lap a broken valve forced him from the race. It was an inauspicious beginning for the season, but at least he proved he could come back. The following night he countered any further doubts about his ability to handle a race car when he drove in a USAC midget race at Manzanita Speedway in Phoenix, Bob Fletcher's hometown. As though to prove to Fletcher he had made a mistake, Jimmy charged home in first place.

After the race that night Jimmy and Suzie went with a group of their friends, including Jerry McClung, to celebrate at a restaurant in South Mountain Pass. Doug came, too, himself recuperating from successful surgery for cancer of the prostate gland. It was 3:00 A.M. before they finished their celebrating, and Jimmy and Doug were so tired they nearly fell asleep. Suzie said to Jerry McClung that night, "Jimmy really needed this one."

The following week Jimmy began radiation therapy again, resuming his daily routine of cobalt treatments each morning. Suzie traveled to Kansas City for the job interview with TWA. A week after her return she received a letter from the airline. She opened it and started reading silently. Jimmy could stand the suspense no longer. "Well, what did they say?" he asked.

"There's good news and bad news," sighed Suzie.

"Okay, Grim, I'll play your game. What's the good news?"

"I'm accepted!"

"Then what could the bad news possibly be?"

"I have to report to training school in May. I'm going to miss the Indy 500 for the first time in fifteen years!"

"Don't worry," Jimmy assured her, laughing. "I'll send you a post card."

Later that night, after Jimmy fell asleep, Suzie lay awake thinking about her new career. It would be glamorous becoming an airline stewardess and she looked forward to it. Once she finished training, she would be able to plan her time-off periods so she could travel to most of Jimmy's races. They might be able to see even more of each other this way. They could use the extra money. And it would be fun.

What she did not like was the idea of leaving Jimmy at this point in his life. Dr. Hauser claimed the radiation was shrinking Jimmy's tumor. He said his cancer was cured. But could they be certain? She might be trading away their last moments together, and this worried her.

What if the cancer came back? She loved him and wanted to be near him. Yet he seemed so delighted and proud of her becoming an airline stewardess. He was like a little kid, happier about her new job than she, almost like a mother bird pushing her young out of the nest to fly and fend for itself. She wanted to stay with Jimmy, and yet she did not want to rob him of the pleasure he obviously attained from making her independent.

What to do? She did not know, except that the decision

already had been made. She would become an airline stewardess. After a while she rolled over and fell asleep.

In mid-April Jimmy encountered Paul Pursell, the physical therapist at Tustin Community Hospital, in the hall. "Hey Paul! What's happening?" he shouted. Jimmy had just come from the X-ray department. His program of radiation had ended; the tests showed no recurrence of any tumor activity; and Dr. Hauser seemed confident that the cancer had been arrested and was receding. Pursell immediately noticed Jimmy's excitement. He looked brighter than at any time during the previous six months.

Jimmy talked about his new racing team and seemed to glow when he spoke about the coming racing season. "I'm really enthusiastic about going to Indy," he told Pursell. "I really think I'm going to do well this year. I feel good physically. I feel good mentally. I'm going to finish right up in front!"

Pursell assumed from Jimmy's conversation, and from what he learned later in talking to members of the hospital staff close to his case, that Jimmy Caruthers' cancer indeed was arrested. He expected he would see him only during the regular six-month intervals when he reported for regular physical exams. Before they parted, Pursell wished him good luck.

"That's what it takes to win at the Speedway," Jimmy conceded.

Yet for a while it appeared that Jimmy Caruthers might not get a chance to drive in the Indianapolis 500. The group responsible for organizing the greatest spectacle in racing is an extremely conservative group, which still felt self-conscious because of the whiplash of public opinion against auto racing caused by the holocaust in 1973. When they received the application for the car that Jimmy Caruthers planned to drive in the 500, they discussed his entry with Dr. David Clutter, the assistant Speedway medical director. "We know Jimmy's a good friend of yours," one of the officials began, "and quite frankly we're concerned about letting him race."

"What's the problem?" asked Dr. Clutter, although he thought he knew what they were angling at.

The official shifted uneasily in his seat. "If Jimmy gets hurt," he said uneasily, "the media is going to jump on our backs again."

"If *anyone* gets hurt, the media will jump on your backs. You know that's the way the press works. How is Jimmy any different?"

"He has cancer."

"So do a lot of people walking around the street," insisted Dr. Clutter. "Some of them know it, some don't. Some have their cancers arrested, others don't. Look, if you tell Jimmy Caruthers he can't race here, you're telling all the other cancer patients in the country they can't live normal lives."

Finally, the official said the Speedway would agree to accept Jimmy Caruthers' entry. As Dr. Clutter started out the door, the official commented to him, "I suppose we've become resigned to the threat of death that comes with our sport. We're used to that. We're not so used to the possibility of death from normal causes."

A thin smile crossed Dr. Clutter's face. "I understand," he said. "I'll express to Jimmy your confidence in his complete recovery."

So Jimmy went to the Speedway in May, again facing, as best he could, the questions of reporters and TV interviewers asking the inevitable question. And Jimmy, if he entertained any inner worries, seemed outwardly cheerful. He kidded about his cancer so others would not feel self-conscious around him. "Hey, don't you know it's the 'in' thing to have cancer?" he joked with Suzie's brother, Bobby, who worked in the Goodyear tire shop at the Speedway.

"The 'in' thing?" Bobby asked, somewhat stunned.

"That's right," Jimmy insisted. "All the important people are getting cancer these days. You really ought to try it."

"Okay, you've sold me," said Bobby, playing along. "How do I start?"

Jimmy pulled a pack of cigarettes out of his pocket, took one, and offered Bobby another.

Those who observed Jimmy Caruthers when he first arrived in the Midwest thought they noticed a change in his driving style from previous years. They thought he looked different sitting in a race car. Jimmy used to hunch over the steering wheel, gripping it tightly. But at Indy in 1975 he looked more relaxed. His head was back, and he seemed nowhere near as tense as before.

Lee Kunzman, however, seemed to feel Jimmy also lost a bit of his safety consciousness. He expressed that belief to several of the other drivers. "I can't put my finger on what makes me feel that way," said Lee. "I just get that impression."

"Maybe Jimmy feels he has nothing to lose," said one of the drivers.

Kunzman considered the possibility that his friend might rather end his life in a race car, falling on his sword so to speak, rather than eaten by some disease. No, Jimmy would never do that, he finally decided. Jimmy knew that if he drove recklessly, it would threaten others around him. His friend was still safety conscious; before, he had been unusually so.

Once a week Jimmy called his mother back in Anaheim. Inevitably she asked how he felt. "Great," he told her. "I haven't felt better in my life. I haven't felt this good in years!"

It was more than mere braggadocio; he actually did feel good. He seemed to possess more stamina than in previous years. It may have been that by relaxing he relieved the tension that previously caused him fatigue. Undergoing treatment for his cancer, he also lost much of the unnecessary weight that once affected his physical conditioning. At one point during the previous year he ballooned to 185 pounds, too much weight for one who stood less than five feet six inches tall. He always blamed Suzie for his weight gain, claiming her cooking was too good. But now his weight was down to 150 pounds.

On the day of the Indy 500 Suzie remained in stewardess training and missed the race. Since Gene Romero was in town, staying at their house, he took her place, hopping on the back of Jimmy's motorcycle when he rode to the track. Burritto planned to serve as Jimmy's board man, signaling him on the track. In Gasoline Alley Jimmy parked the motorcycle near his garage. "Aren't you going to kiss me?" he asked.

"What are you talking about?"

"Suzie always kissed me before I went racing," Jimmy grinned.

"Suzie did a lot of things with you that I don't plan to do."

At the TWA training center for stewardesses in Dallas Suzie listened to the broadcast of the race on radio. Back at Tustin Community Hospital many of the employees on duty that afternoon also listened by radio to find out how their former patient was doing.

A number of minor problems plagued Jimmy throughout the race. A faulty magneto caused his ignition to misfire and made him lose several laps because of extra pit stops. The oil tank behind him overheated and bothered his back. He finally asked his pit crew to put extra padding in the seat for protection against heat. Even with these problems he moved into the top ten by the 174th lap, when it began to rain so heavily that the drivers could barely see. The yellow light came on, cautioning them to slow down, but the starter hesitated to throw the red flag, which would officially stop the race. Even if he had stopped it, nobody would have seen the flag because the downpour limited visibility to twenty yards.

Coming down the front straightaway in the pouring rain, Bill Puterbaugh slowed to about twenty-five miles per hour and attempted to turn into the pits. But his car almost was floating. He skidded sideways in front of Jimmy. Jimmy tried to avoid the other driver, first turning his steering wheel; then, when that didn't work, stomping on the brakes. He barely stopped in time. But another race car, driven by Bently Warren, coming up from behind, slid into hìm. The crash did not injure Jimmy, but it damaged his car. Jimmy climbed out and walked back to the garage with Burritto, both of them soaked in the pouring rain. "Man, that was like driving a boat without a rudder," Jimmy said. "They get up on that water and you can't steer them."

Unable to cross the finish line because of the accident, Jimmy's race position dropped to fourteenth place.

His car was too badly damaged to drive at Milwaukee the following weekend, but it was ready for him to race in the Pocono 500 at the end of June. Before Pocono, he took his midget to a race at Penn National Speedway. He qualified but had problems with the car and could not run the heat race or the semifeature. For the main event he started in last position, obtaining the starting spot only as a fill-in for another driver. The track was dirt, packed hard but dotted with ruts and holes, the kind of track where driving skill can overcome machinery. Jimmy came darting through the field, taking cars high, taking them low, doing everything except leaping over them in his move to the front. He finally took the checkered flag in first place. His father was stunned by the performance. He felt it was the best race he had ever seen Jimmy run.

In addition to racing championship cars and midgets, Jimmy also began entering stock car races, and even drove sprint cars, which surprised Lee Kunzman. "You never liked driving sprint cars before," Lee commented to his friend. "Why are you doing it now?"

Jimmy shrugged off the question. "I've got a lot of hospital bills."

Lee wondered whether this was his actual motive. In racing four and five times a week, often renting private planes to fly from one race to another, Jimmy almost spent more money than he could earn. It seemed almost as though he had a compulsion to prove cancer had not slowed him down or affected his ability as a driver. Or maybe he was trying to squeeze as much living as possible into his last days.

In mid July the USAC midget drivers headed west for a series of races in the Rocky Mountain area. Jimmy rented a plane and flew west along with Johnny Parsons, Jr., and Pancho Carter. They raced in Meridian, Idaho, one night, in Provo, Utah, the next night, and two nights later appeared in Erie, Colorado, outside Denver. "The last USAC race Danny ever won in his life was in Denver," Jimmy commented to his friends.

Jimmy previously made arrangements for his ex-wife to bring his son to Denver. He looked forward to seeing young Jimmy. At the last moment, however, she called to cancel the plans. Parsons noticed that Jimmy seemed extremely disappointed. Jimmy Caruthers won the race near Denver. Afterwards, they headed back to the Midwest.

Jimmy reported to Dr. David Clutter for a physical examination, partly to satisfy Federal Aviation Agency requirements that cancer patients have physicals once every six months. Dr. Clutter examined Jimmy's X-rays and said he noticed no activity in the tumor area, but he mailed the negatives to Dr. Hauser in California to confirm his diagnosis. Johnny Parsons, Jr., came with Jimmy to the doctor's office and afterwards the two drivers went with Dave Clutter to a nearby restaurant called Friday's.

Later, the manager stopped by their table. It was Thursday, and every Thursday at midnight Friday's staged a celebration in honor of the next day. Friday began the weekend—"Thank God, it's Friday!"—which was the reason for the restaurant's name. The manager explained they usually staged wild happenings in connection with their midnight celebrations, and wondered if they would like to return that night. In fact, would they like to stage something? Jimmy decided they would have a bicycle race through the restaurant, and since Gene Romero also happened to be in town, invited him and several motorcycle buddies to attend. That evening, while nearly 600 patrons of the restaurant cheered, Caruthers, Parsons, Burritto, and several others raced bicycles around the inside of the restaurant, knocking over tables, chairs, and otherwise having a wild time. One biker even rode a motorcycle through the restaurant, almost starting a fire.

Jimmy frequently went flying during the summer. Pancho Carter and Dave Clutter both were learning to fly, and he often went up with them. One weekend stunt pilot Art Scholl came into town and took Jimmy for a ride. Scholl, one of the top aerobatic pilots in the world, does a stunt in which he lets the plane fall out of control. The plane flutters wheel over tail until finally, at the last moment, Scholl pulls the plane up before hitting the ground. It is a stunt that only a handful of pilots dare attempt. Scholl did the stunt one afternoon with Jimmy in the plane.

"Three-two-one, Conkle," said Jimmy after Scholl pulled out of the spin.

"What's that?" asked Scholl.

"That's just like heading down the main straightaway at Indianapolis."

Lee Kunzman worried because his friend went continuously from one race to another, never pausing. "Why don't you rest for a while?" Lee asked him when they were out one night. "You're running practically every night of the week. You can't travel and stay awake as long as you do and cram as much as you do into every minute and stay mentally and physically alert."

"I feel great," Jimmy insisted. "I'm doing what I want to do. What else is more important?"

10

A reporter asked Jimmy Caruthers at the start of the summer of 1975 to name the form of auto racing he enjoyed most, ignoring the normal considerations of fame and fortune: "If you were racing just for the pure joy of the sport, what kind of car would you most want to drive?"

It was not an easy question, and Jimmy took a long time to answer it. He considered the excellence of the championship cars, their being such expensive and well engineered machines that rush through the corners with speed that even he found hard to comprehend. He liked the precision of championship cars.

He thought about the wild, wheel-banging that was possible when you drove midget racers, the way drivers ran so close to each other, running in packs of five or six cars, swapping positions constantly. He liked the quickness of the midgets.

He did not care much for stock cars, which he considered heavy to drive, and for which brute strength seemed more important than skill. He disliked sprint cars for another reason. They were overpowered, too jumpy, too nervous, and therefore too dangerous. They scared him.

Finally he decided he liked dirt cars the best. "Dirt cars are neat," Jimmy explained, "because they are big and fast and are my favorite kind of racing to watch. They rush into the corner, go into a long drag slide, end up against the fence, and come out sprinkling rubber, dirt, mud, and everything up into the crowd." He laughed, then added, "I guess everybody likes to do best what they do best, and I've had good luck with dirt cars. I'm looking forward to running the dirt cars this season."

Jimmy Caruthers also liked driving dirt cars because his boyhood idol, Jimmy Bryan, had been such a master of the breed. The average race fan remembers Bryan because he once won Indianapolis, but those within the racing fraternity, the people who travel the circuit, remember Bryan best because of his exploits on dirt. Back in the fifties the same cars that raced at Indy—the roadsters—also ran on dirt, and Bryan seemed particularly adept on such tracks.

On paved tracks a driver's success depends a great deal on the ability of his automobile. Drivers who work for well-financed teams tend to win races. But on dirt tracks—which sometimes are loose, sometimes are hard, but always are bumpy—the driver is more responsible for his own fate. Bryan knew how to pick his way around a dirt track, no matter what the surface conditions, and find the fast line to victory.

But after rear-engine race cars became popular at Indy during the mid-sixties, late model championship cars no longer raced on dirt tracks. They were a completely different kind of car—low-slung, light, finely balanced, not meant to handle well on bumpy ground. Driving a championship car on a dirt track would be like driving a Cadillac on a pack trail. You just did not do it anymore.

The dirt tracks, at least the ones large enough to accommodate the bigger cars, began to disappear one by one. They either went out of business or were paved so they could accommodate the Indy cars. By the mid-seventies, only a handful of mile-long dirt tracks remained at fair grounds in DuQuoin, Syracuse, Springfield, and Indianapolis. The USAC conducted only four or five races each year in the division. Yet the dirt car championship ranked nearly equal in prestige to most of the other USAC division championships. It was a division Jimmy Caruthers enjoyed driving in and one in which he wanted to win. Doug maintained a dirt car specifically so his son could compete each year in the series.

Several other cars, however, were more competitive, particularly one campaigned by George Middleton, owner of the Pizza Hut franchise in St. Louis. He owned the car formerly driven by A. J. Foyt. In addition, Middleton had an excellent mechanic named Larry Griffith, who prepared his car. During the winter Middleton and Griffith talked to Jimmy about driving the car, but Jimmy seemed reluctant to abandon his father's car. Hanging over his head, also, was the question of whether or not his cancer would prevent him from competing. He had been told he was cured—but are you ever "cured?" Middleton and Griffith also spoke to Bobby Unser, who showed interest in the car, but eventually admitted that an exclusive contract with Dan Gurney prevented him from running anything but championship cars without Gurney's permission, which was not forthcoming.

Middleton and Griffith did not give up. At a midget race in Springfield, Illinois, in June, Doug was working on his car when Larry Griffith approached, somewhat timidly: "We'd like to have Jimmy run for us, but we don't want to make you mad."

Doug laughed. "That don't make me mad," he said. "I'd like to see him drive your car. He'll win the championship for you."

Griffith later spoke to Jimmy, who, after warming up his midget, rolled into the pits to discuss the possible change with his father. "Hey, those guys asked me to drive their car."

"Yeah, I've already talked to them," Doug admitted.

"Well, what do you think?"

"Go ahead and drive it."

"Who's going to drive yours?"

"I can get anybody to drive mine."

So at the first dirt car race at Syracuse, New York, on the fourth of July, Jimmy Caruthers drove the Pizza Hut car, while Bill Puterbaugh drove his father's machine. Jimmy qualified in sixteenth place, but by the end of the 100-mile event he had moved up to fourth place behind Sheldon Kinser, Arnie Knepper, and Pancho Carter. Puterbaugh failed to finish because of a punctured tire.

Afterwards, Jimmy commented to one of his friends, "I can see why Foyt got rid of the car," he commented. "It doesn't handle all that well and doesn't run fast." He weighed the car's liabilities against its assets. "But it runs strong. It really runs strong. I can finish races with it, but I'll probably never win one."

Six weeks passed before the second dirt car race on August 16 in Springfield, Illinois. Middleton and Griffith arrived at the track early, ready to race, but Jimmy, who had to practice for a championship car race the following day in Milwaukee, was absent. As race time approached, Larry Griffith feared his driver might not make it. He asked Ralph Liguori to help warm up the car. Only minutes before qualifications began, Jimmy drove up with a big grin on his face: "I'll bet you didn't think I was going to get here, did you?"

Jimmy qualified eighth, but placed second behind Al Unser. After the race the crowd poured out of the stands and surged around Jimmy for autographs. The temperature was nearly 100 degrees, and the grueling 100-lap race had exhausted Jimmy. He could have begged off, insisting he had to run the following day in Milwaukee, but he stood in the pits for nearly two hours, signing autographs and talking, until the last fan left the track.

At Milwaukee on Sunday he placed sixth in the championship car event, but his back bothered him. He asked Johnny Capels to put extra padding into the cockpit of the car, but it did not seem to help. After the race he telephoned his mother in California and admitted having back pains. "They're different from last summer," he admitted. "They're sharp pains, more like a knife." Earlier that summer Jimmy flipped his sprint car. The car bounced off its nose and landed hard on all four wheels. He speculated this might have caused the new back pains.

He called Dave Clutter while still in Milwaukee. "My back is killing me," he said.

"Tell me about it," suggested the doctor.

Jimmy described the pains as sharp. "You remember that overheating problem we had at Indy this year?" he commented. "When I got out of the cockpit, my back was red as a beet. Maybe that started something."

"Could be," mused the doctor, "but I doubt it."

Jimmy paused, as though unwilling to say what was on his mind. Finally he blurted it out: "I was worried that the back pains might be related to my problems last winter."

"That's not the sort of diagnosis I would want to make on the telephone," said Dr. Clutter. "Why don't you hustle back to Indianapolis for an examination."

Jimmy returned immediately, but a thorough checkup failed to reveal any activity in the tumor area. Dr. Clutter took X-rays again and forwarded them to California. He spoke later by telephone with Dr. Hauser, who said, "The clips attached to the original tumor haven't moved."

"Then there's no further activity there."

"As near as I can determine from these X-rays," conceded the California surgeon.

Dr. Clutter replaced the receiver on its cradle, sat with his hand still resting on it while he considered various options, then dialed Jimmy's number. Jimmy was at home and answered the phone. "The clip positions indicate the original tumor remains shrunken," Dr. Clutter told him.

"That's good news," said Jimmy.

"In the sense that no news is good news," conceded Dr. Clutter. "We still don't know what's bothering your back."

"Well, maybe it was that sprint car accident after all," Jimmy rationalized.

"Maybe," said the doctor, unconvinced.

Jimmy hung up the telephone. He later called Suzie to discuss plans for her to be at his next race. She had completed stewardess training and was on reserve duty for TWA, flying out of O'Hare Field near Chicago. Befitting her low seniority, it was the least desirable assignment for an airline stewardess. If another stewardess had to miss a flight, someone on reserve replaced her. On the days she was on call she had to remain near the telephone. The airline might call and send her anywhere in the country on short notice. But after flying a certain number of hours she received time off, sometimes as much as seven or eight consecutive days if she planned her schedule well. While flying stand-by, she shared an apartment in suburban Mount Prospect, near the airport, with two other stewardesses. Whenever possible, she returned to Indianapolis, or wherever Jimmy was racing.

"What about those back pains you've been having?" she asked him.

"Dr. Clutter says they're because of my sprint car accident."

The third dirt car race came the following weekend in Du Quoin, Illinois. Car owner George Middleton, realiz-

ing that championships in auto racing go to those who survive more often than to those who take risks, ordered mechanic Larry Griffith not to run their engine at more than
8,800 revolutions per minute. At such relatively low rpm's,
the car would produce less power at the end of the
straightaway, but would also be less likely to suffer engine
failure. Larry and Jimmy, however, discussed the engine's
capabilities and decided it could be run safely at much
higher rpm's. They neglected to tell Middleton, however.

The tachometer in their car had a "telltale" needle that
indicated maximum rpm's, but every time Jimmy wound
the engine past 8,800, he hit the kickback button, returning the needle to zero. Middleton began nosing around
the cockpit, suspicious of what sounded like excessive revolutions, but unable to prove it. One time Jimmy forgot to
hit the kickback button, and Middleton was stunned by
what he saw.

"My Gawd! Ninety-four hundred rpm's!"

Jimmy glanced at the dial and shrugged, "Must have hit
a hole in the track and spun my wheels."

"Relax, George," Larry Griffith told the car owner and
suggested that he watch the race from the stands. Middleton accepted the suggestion humbly, but walked off, mut-
tering about how many pizzas he would have to sell to replace the engine if it exploded.

As it happened, the engine did not explode, but a brake
plate disintegrated at forty miles and Jimmy drove the last
sixty miles of the race without brakes. He still finished
fourth, despite having qualified only sixteenth fastest.

At St. Paul, Minnesota, the following weekend, despite
its being a "dirt car" series, they raced on a half-mile paved
track. Larry Griffith tried some new, softer tires, hoping to
improve their usually poor qualifying position. The tires
failed to help. Jimmy went out and qualified eighteenth.
"What happened?" Larry asked him.

Jimmy refused to alibi. "I just tried too hard," he claimed.

However, Larry decided the blame for the poor qualification time belonged to the soft tires. They worked well during hot-lapping because Jimmy had enough time on the track to raise their temperature and "melt" the rubber so the tires gripped the track. But while they waited in the pits to qualify, the tires cooled off and lost much of their adhesive quality.

The Pizza Hut car typically qualified poorly because of its soft suspension, a poor set-up on a smooth track. But usually, as the races continued, the track got harder and bumpier and slicker (from oil drippings) and the soft suspension proved superior at the end.

Before the St. Paul race Jimmy worried he might have trouble finishing. It was another hot day. Because the track was only a half mile, he would need to drive 200 laps, negotiating 400 turns, to cover the 100-mile distance. "I haven't been eating good lately," he admitted to Griffith. "I might have trouble going the distance."

Jimmy asked Johnny Parsons, Jr., to stand by, ready to relieve him: "When I get tired, I'll pat myself on the top of the helmet. I'll come in about ten laps after that. Be ready to jump in the car."

After Jimmy climbed into his cockpit, however, Parsons took Griffith aside. "Do you usually flash Jimmy signals on the pit board?"

"Now and then," Larry admitted.

"What you should do is keep flashing Jimmy information all during the race. If you keep his mind occupied, he'll forget how tired he is and finish."

Having qualified eighteenth, Jimmy started the race nearly a half lap behind Tom Bigelow, who had the fastest qualifying time. As the race wore on and the track got slicker, Jimmy moved steadily toward the front. Meanwhile, one of Bigelow's tires began blistering, raising doubt whether he could finish. Larry kept flashing Jimmy information on the pit board as he moved closer and closer to the front. His driver still had not patted his helmet to indicate he wanted relief from Parsons.

Finally, Jimmy moved into second place and began to narrow the gap between him and Bigelow, whose tire continued to blister. But the checkered flag fell, with Bigelow the winner and Jimmy still six seconds behind. Jimmy crossed the finish line in second and slowed his car. As he rounded turn four on the cool-down lap and cruised into the pits, he reached overhead and patted his helmet, indicating he was tired and wanted relief. Griffith and Parsons had to lift him out of the cockpit. "I never saw a guy run so gallant a race before," Larry commented later, tears in his eyes.

That evening the Pizza Hut team sat around the motel and had a quiet celebration. With only one race remaining on the dirt-car circuit, Jimmy led in points for the championship. He had not yet won a single race, but his steady finishes (two fourths and two seconds) put him well ahead of Tom Bigelow, who, while winning two races, had placed eleventh in two others.

"What makes a super racer?" asked Larry Griffith during the night.

"Probably vision," Jimmy replied.

Larry thought that interesting since Jimmy Caruthers wore eyeglasses while he raced. In fact, Clint Brawner once blamed Jimmy's early problems in championship cars on a lack of depth perception. Brawner felt Jimmy improved as a driver only when he began wearing glasses. A number of other drivers, including Mike Mosely and Joe Leonard, also wore glasses, but usually donned them only at the last minute to keep that knowledge from the fans who did not like their heroes flawed—or so the drivers thought.

"I used to fly helicopters at Riverside Raceway," Jimmy

explained. While still young, he ferried race drivers from the Los Angeles airport to the track. One time he picked up British driver Jimmy Clark, arriving for a Grand Prix race. "I was astounded at his vision. He could look off in the distance and read freeway signs that I couldn't even see."

There was a sudden lull in the conversation as each one in the room retreated into his own thoughts. Jimmy Clark won the Indy 500 in 1965, the first driver ever to do so in a rear-engined car. Two years later he died in his race car. Even his superior vision could not protect him.

Jimmy slept uneasily that night, not because of memories of Clark, but because he could not get comfortable. He tried rolling over in different positions. If it was not his back, it was his stomach. If it was not his stomach, it was his chest. And his arms ached from the effort of wrestling a heavy dirt car through two hundred turns. He finally fell asleep, but woke up early, still feeling exhausted.

Several days later he called Dr. Hauser in California. "I'm having some discomfort," he admitted.

"Is your back still bothering you?" the surgeon quizzed him.

"Yes, but—" he hesitated.

"But what?"

"I also have some pains in my right chest." He added, "My stomach seems bloated."

"We probably should take a look at you."

Jimmy agreed, but did not seem anxious to leave the Midwest. He stalled for time. "I've got a couple of more races to run, then I'll be home."

Later that night Jimmy talked long distance to Suzie. He failed to mention his conversation with Dr. Hauser.

The final dirt car race of the season was the Hoosier Hundred at the Indiana State Fairgrounds in Indianapolis on September 6. Suzie planned her schedule so she could be home that weekend. Jimmy qualified fifth, his best starting position, but trouble loomed. During the St. Paul race the harmonic balancer in the engine had cracked. This caused damage to the oil seal that went undetected until after the Hoosier Hundred qualifications. They had to replace the oil seal immediately, although such repairs are not effectively done at the track.

Johnny Capels, Jimmy's championship car mechanic, who was helping in the pits that day, rushed to his shop to obtain a replacement seal. They quickly made the repair, but worried about its effectiveness. Larry Griffith believed that with oil leaking out of the car, it would not last a full hundred laps. Assuming Bigelow won the race, Jimmy would need to finish at least fifth to guarantee himself the championship.

Another car owner offered his car, but Jimmy declined, "I've come this far with this car. I'll finish the season with it, one way or the other."

Larry took his driver aside before the start of the final event. "Jim, you've got to keep the r's down, or the engine won't go a hundred miles."

Jimmy grinned, "No fooling with the kickback button?"

"No fooling with the kickback button."

"Then I'll just run it steady as long as it will go."

Larry Griffith was impressed with the calm manner in which Jimmy Caruthers accepted the impending disaster. He thought that most drivers would get upset and throw things.

Almost from the moment the green flag dropped, signaling the start of the race, smoke billowed from behind the Pizza Hut car, the effect of oil dripping onto the hot engine. Four drivers had qualified ahead of Jimmy—Johnny Parsons, Jr., Bill Engelhart, Sheldon Kinser, and James McElreath. One by one they dropped out—but Bigelow and A. J. Foyt came charging up from behind. Jimmy found he could run even with Bigelow through the corners and down the straightaway until the point where his engine reached 7,800 rpm's. Then he eased off the throttle to preserve the engine.

At the end of one hundred laps Jimmy's engine was still smoking—and still running. After he pulled into the pits, Larry Griffith checked the level in Jimmy's oil tank. He found it was bone-dry. "Another two or three laps and the engine would have frozen," whistled Larry.

But if's don't count in auto racing. By finishing third, Jimmy Caruthers won his second USAC championship. Almost the moment the last car engine died, Suzie Grim came running down from her seat in the grandstand, brushed past the track guards, crossed the pitted and dusty track, and rushed into the pits to throw her arms around Jimmy. For a long, long time they stood there, hugging each other, not saying a word. There were tears in Suzie's eyes. "You did it, Jimmy," she finally gasped.

"I feel terrific."

"You did it," she repeated.

"I've never been happier in my life," he told her. They continued holding on to each other until the crush of others wanting interviews and autographs forced them apart.

That night they attended a party at the home of car builder A. J. Watson. Jimmy had a midget car race to drive the following day in Terre Haute, so he made Suzie promise to drag him out of the party at midnight no matter how much he wanted to stay. "Use force if necessary," he insisted.

Promptly at midnight she told him, "Jimmy, we've got to go."

They started for the door, but he kept getting stopped by people congratulating him on his triumph. It took them another half hour before they finally got outside.

The next morning they awoke early to leave for Terre Haute. "Thanks for making me leave," Jimmy told Suzie.

"How do you feel?" she asked.

"I feel great," he told her. "I've never felt better in my life."

11

At the championship car race in Michigan the following weekend Dennis Woods, who handled public relations for Fletcher Racing, was walking through the garage area when he heard somebody yell "Hey, Woods!"

He turned and saw Jimmy Caruthers. Jimmy sat on a tractor outside the garage housing his race car. Dennis stopped and chatted briefly with the driver, and the subject of Jimmy's health came up, as it so often did in conversations that summer with friends. Woods wanted to know how Jimmy felt.

"Hey, I feel good," boasted Jimmy. "I'll be going back to California in a couple of weeks for some more checks."

Woods prodded for more information: "Honest? Do you really feel good?"

Jimmy laughed and spread his arms as though to indicate that his presence at the racetrack was proof of his health. "Hey, Woods," he said. "I'm racing!"

Jimmy Caruthers was racing extremely well, too. After

having been hit from behind at Indianapolis, damaging his team's only car and causing him to miss the Milwaukee race two weeks later, Jimmy Caruthers finished every race, following on the championship trail. He placed eighth at Pocono in June, seventh at Michigan in July, and sixth at Milwaukee in August.

The Morales team did not have the finances to permit him to run up front with the top drivers, but he consistently ran hard. With a little more experience and with additional financial backing, it looked at though next year Jimmy Caruthers could be running up with the front runners instead of just behind them.

Jimmy placed fourth at Michigan. He returned to Indianapolis between that race and the one in Trenton, New Jersey, the following weekend. During the week his mother called from California. Jimmy's son was spending the day at her home and wanted to talk to his father. Jimmy spent nearly ten minutes on the phone with him. "Daddy, I miss you," said young Jimmy. "I wish you could come home."

"I'll be coming home in another week," Jimmy promised.

In Trenton he placed seventh and caught an immediate flight to California, arriving in Los Angeles after two A.M. His mother met him at the airport. He stayed that night at her house.

When he awoke Monday morning Jimmy called Dr. Hauser's office and made an appointment for later that afternoon. He stopped by Don Edmunds' shop and the two of them went to lunch. Edmunds thought his friend looked tired, subdued. The car builder was preparing seven midget race cars to run indoors in the Midwest in January, and they talked about plans for the races, but only for a few minutes. Then Jimmy changed the subject and began talking about other things.

That afternoon, when Dr. Hauser examined him in his

office, Jimmy described a fullness after eating. Dr. Hauser felt his abdomen and found it soft, with no evidence of any obstruction similar to the tumor he found last December. As the doctor pressed down on his rib cage, Jimmy complained that it felt tender.

"Maybe I cracked something in that sprint car accident a couple of months ago," suggested Jimmy.

Dr. Hauser shook his head. "I wouldn't count on that." He sent Jimmy across the street to the hospital to have X-rays taken of his rib cage and adbomen.

In the X-ray department Jimmy met Joe Aldenhifer, the technician and auto buff whom he had gotten to know on previous visits to Tustin Community Hospital. While taking X-rays, Aldenhifer chatted with Jimmy and asked what he thought was bothering him. Jimmy mentioned his sore ribs. "I think I'm getting bruised in the race car going around those tight turns. Maybe the g's are getting to me."

"Yeah," said Aldenhifer. "That's probably what's wrong."

The following morning Jimmy called Dr. Hauser to inquire about the results of the X-rays. The doctor noted that the clips still remained together, indicating no recurrence of the tumor. The mass was smaller than the previous spring.

But two days later, on Thursday night, Jimmy felt stomach pains after he ate. He called Dr. Hauser the next day. The surgeon suggested he return for a more complete diagnosis. Jimmy began to stall: "I've got some business I have to take care of."

"The sooner you come in, the quicker we can diagnose your problem," suggested Dr. Hauser.

"I'll come in as soon as I get things squared away."

"I'm concerned about this, Jimmy," warned Dr. Hauser. "I want to hear from you."

"I'll keep in touch."

"I want to know if your stomach gets any worse or if you have other problems."

That weekend the city of Long Beach sponsored a Formula 5000 race through the city streets, a prelude to a Grand Prix race scheduled the following season for Formula One cars. Jimmy did not drive in the race, but attended practice and qualifications Friday and Saturday, then caught a late afternoon flight to Buffalo, New York.

Recently he had obtained an appointment as member of the Champion Spark Plug Highway Safety Team, a group of drivers who visited high schools during the winter to talk about safe driving. It paid good money off season and many drivers coveted the assignment as a plum. Jimmy attended training sessions at company headquarters in Toledo that summer, but had not yet made any personal appearances because of the school vacation period. Driver Bob Harkey met him in Buffalo to assist him during his first few appearances. Later, as he became more experienced, Jimmy would travel alone. They planned to visit several high schools toward the end of the week. Jimmy expected to return to the West Coast for a USAC midget race in San Bernardino on Friday night, October 3.

Harkey noticed that Jimmy seemed to have trouble eating. "What's the matter?" he asked.

"Lost my appetite, I guess," said Jimmy. Actually, Jimmy's stomach had become badly bloated, almost like a watermelon. It was hard. He cancelled his school appearances and returned to the West Coast one day early, stopping briefly in Chicago to visit Suzie.

On Friday Jimmy saw Dr. Hauser, who suggested he check into the hospital so they could drain the fluid from his stomach. "I've got a race to run tonight," begged Jimmy. Dr. Hauser agreed to let him check into the hospital the next day.

When Jimmy went to the garage to get the race car

ready, he discovered his stomach was so bloated he could not fit comfortably into the cockpit. His stomach got in the way of the steering wheel. He called promoter J. C. Agajanian and apologized, saying he was sick and unable to compete. "I know you advertised that I would be there, Aggie, but I just can't make it."

Aggie suggested that if Jimmy decided to attend the race as a spectator, he should stop by the press box so they could make an announcement. "That will satisfy the crowd," said Aggie. Jimmy promised to do so.

That evening he took his young son with him to the track. George Snider also appeared to apologize for his absence, having broken an arm in a sprint car accident. Rosie Rosenhof, the track announcer, interviewed both drivers over the public address system while waiting for the feature race. He asked how he felt.

"I'm okay," Jimmy answered. "I felt a little bad today. I checked in with my doctor, and they want to run a few tests."

"You had some bad luck about a year ago," suggested Rosie. "Does it have anything to do with that?"

"I had some surgery last year," Jimmy conceded. "I'm having some trouble around the incision. Something about adhesions."

"Everybody is expecting you to be at the Turkey race. Are you going to be there?"

"I plan to be. The doctor thinks everything is okay, but he wants to run some tests. I'm checking into the hospital tomorrow, but should be out by Tuesday. I'm planning to run the Turkey Night."

After the interview Jimmy remained in the booth for a while to talk to some of his friends. J. C. Agajanian noticed that Jimmy reached in his pocket for a cigarette. When he lit it, Aggie said, "Jimmy, why not get rid of those cigarettes? You don't have to smoke."

Jimmy turned and smiled at him, "Yeah, I'm going to quit one of these days."

Early Saturday morning Jimmy checked into the hospital. Dr. Hauser slipped a trocar into his abdominal cavity and drained the fluid present. A pathologist checked the fluid and Dr. Hauser returned to Jimmy's room with the results of the tests. He came right to the point: "We've got trouble again."

"What's wrong?"

"Your cancer has recurred."

"Fine," groaned Jimmy. "Just what I've always wanted."

"The fluid drained from your stomach contains cancer cells," Dr. Hauser continued, "very active cancer cells."

"You're positive?"

Dr. Hauser mentioned the names of two other physicians with whom he had discussed the diagnosis. One was pathologist Dr. Calvin Marantz, who had taken the samples. The other was Dr. Irving Drumm, a specialist in chemotherapy for cancer patients.* "They suspect that the cancer recurred as another form of testicular tumor."

"The same thing I had last year?"

"Not quite the same."

"I suppose this means more radiation treatments," sighed Jimmy. He did not anticipate with pleasure a return to cobalt therapy and its side effects.

"I'm not sure we want to do that again," said the surgeon.

"Then what?"

"I don't know," admitted Dr. Hauser. "That's one of the problems with cancer. We don't know all the answers. There's also a possibility that the malignancy may have

*Irving Drumm, M.D., is a pseudonym for a physician who has insisted that his actual identity not be revealed. He is the only individual in this book whose real name is not given.

spread into your liver. We want to do more tests beginning Monday."

Jimmy frowned. "Not until Monday?" He said he wanted to attend a motorcycle race at Ontario on Sunday. Dr. Hauser gave him permission to attend, but asked him to report back to the hospital Sunday night so the further tests could begin the next morning. Jimmy promised to return.

On his way out he encountered physical therapist Paul Pursell. More from a conversational nature, Pursell asked him how things were going.

"My stomach has been bugging me," Jimmy said.

"That's too bad," commented Pursell. "What's wrong?"

"It looks like my tumor's kicking up again."

Paul Pursell mumbled a few words of encouragement but did not want to hash over Jimmy's medical history in the hallway. He remarked later to others in the hospital that Jimmy Caruthers seemed disappointed, dazed, almost as though he had run into a brick wall.

Shortly after Jimmy arrived at his La Palma apartment, the telephone rang. It was Suzie. She was scheduled that afternoon to fly from Indianapolis to Los Angeles, with an overnight layover before returning to Chicago, and Jimmy planned to pick her up at the airport. She called to say her plane had mechanical difficulties and she would be several hours late. "What did the doctors say?" she asked.

"We'll talk about it when you get out here," said Jimmy.

"Don't do that to me, Jimmy. I've got a four-hour flight. Tell me what the doctors said!"

"I've got Big C again."

"Where?"

"They don't know yet. They think maybe my liver."

Jimmy went to a restaurant with his mother for dinner. With his stomach drained of fluid, his appetite had returned and he ordered steak. After dinner he bought a copy of Sunday's Los Angeles *Times* to check the classified ads. "Pancho and I are thinking of going in together on an airplane," he explained.

Even as Jimmy said those words he began to think of the reality he faced beyond that dream. The recurrence of his cancer meant more medical treatment and more bills. His hope of purchasing an airplane seemed further and further away.

When Suzie's plane landed, Jimmy met her at the airport. They drove to the Airport Marina Motel, where the TWA crews stayed between flights in Los Angeles. They sat around the motel that evening, talking. Jimmy described how they stuck a needle into his stomach to drain the fluid. It was very painful and his stomach still hurt. Suzie thought it sounded dreadful.

That night, after they went to bed, Suzie lay with her back to him. She was almost asleep when she felt the pressure of Jimmy's forehead pressed lightly against her bare back, as though a sign of affection. It was uncharacteristic of him, something he normally would not do. She thought he must be very worried. She fell asleep with his forehead still pressed against her back.

Suzie flew to Chicago early the next morning. Jimmy took his son to the motorcycle races at the Ontario Motor Speedway. Burritto was racing that day and he spent time with him in the pits. Joe Scalzo, an auto racing writer, was walking through the tunnel under the track to catch the elevator up to the press box when he noticed Jimmy. He had not seen him for ten months, and Jimmy had lost so much weight that Scalzo almost failed to recognize him. Scalzo finally asked, "How's Burritto doing?"

"He's having trouble with his bike," Jimmy responded.

Scalzo paused, momentarily uncertain whether or not the person before him was the right man. "You are Jimmy Caruthers, aren't you?"

"Yeah, I'm Jimmy Caruthers."

In the press box he met Denny Bender, a public relations man with the Champion Spark Plug Company who wanted Jimmy to say hello to some customers being entertained at the race. Afterwards, Jimmy pulled Bender to one side and mentioned his current medical problems, but only admitted to having "tests." Jimmy wanted to know if the health insurance he now had as a member of the Champion Spark Plug Highway Safety Team would cover his hospital bills?

"I'm not sure, Jimmy," Bender admitted. "They might consider what you have a prior illness."

"That's what I was afraid of," said Jimmy, "but check anyway, just in case I'm covered."

Bender promised to do so and Jimmy assured him he would be able to fulfill a scheduled assignment in Albany, New York, later that month.

After the day's racing, Jimmy returned his son to his ex-wife and then went to visit his mother. Feeling tired, he lay down to rest. After a short nap he awoke and drove his car to the hospital. The next morning he began the series of tests designed to pinpoint the location of his cancer. He had an upper GI series as well as a bone scan and brain scan.

Dr. Hauser checked the test results later that day. They showed the entire abdominal area to be studded with tumor cells. These cells provided the irritant that caused fluid to form within Jimmy's stomach as a means of coating them with a protective layer. Although the original tumor remained shrunken, another tumor mass was now discovered behind the stomach and in a higher area than the previous one. Apparently the tumor treated with cobalt rays the previous winter had metastasized, changing into another, more malignant form of cancer than the pure seminoma originally diagnosed. Or perhaps the other cells were present a year ago but had remained undetected. It meant Jimmy's battle with cancer was not yet finished.

Dr. Hauser stopped by his patient's room to inform him of the diagnosis. "Sounds pretty bad," Jimmy admitted.

"I've been in touch with Dr. Drumm," Dr. Hauser explained. "He's a specialist in chemotherapy."

"Chemotherapy?"

"Treating cancer with drugs. Chemicals. He thinks there's a fairly good chance of arresting the disease."

After Dr. Hauser left, Jimmy called Dave Clutter in Indianapolis. "Hey, what does it mean to have metastatic disease?"

Dr. Clutter explained that the malignancy must have changed from one form to another, but admitted that cancer was out of his field.

"Dr. Hauser claims he has a good chance of curing me with chemotherapy," Jimmy continued. "What do you think?"

"Well, if that's what Dr. Hauser said, I'd believe him."

After Jimmy hung up, Dave Clutter pulled down several medical books from his library shelf. After he finished reading, he began to worry for his friend. It was not like the original seminoma, where they had one primary tumor on which they could concentrate. Metastatic tumors were much more difficult to isolate and treat, and it seemed, from what he read, very unlikely that Jimmy could survive this latest complication in his case. He picked up the telephone and called Dr. Hauser to obtain more detailed information on Jimmy's disease. Dr. Hauser, however, seemed optimistic. "I think we can lick it with drugs," the surgeon explained.

Dr. Clutter hung up the telephone, feeling more comfortable, but he still worried that Jimmy Caruthers might soon be dead.

Over the weekend Shirley Fitzpatrick talked with her mother-in-law. Mrs. Maxine Fitzpatrick had attended the midget races at San Bernardino Friday night and had seen Jimmy Caruthers. She did not speak to him, but he sat in the stands nearby with his son.

Mrs. Fitzpatrick, who admitted a low tolerance for noisy children, told Shirley how impressed she was with the manner in which Jimmy disciplined his son. The boy began to act a bit rambunctious, as young children will, and Jimmy spoke harshly to his son once. After that the boy caused no more trouble for the remainder of the evening.

What also impressed Mrs. Fitzpatrick was how sick Jimmy looked. "Has his cancer returned?" she asked her daughter-in-law. Shirley could not say. She knew from the other technicians that Jimmy Caruthers recently had some more X-rays taken, but she had not seen him herself.

On Monday morning Shirley encountered Jimmy in the hospital corridor. It was their first meeting since last spring, and Shirley noticed how much weight he had lost, though she said nothing. Remembering her pregnancy, he asked about the new baby. Shirley said she and Jack had a boy and named him Ryan Fitzpatrick.

"You didn't name him after a race driver then?" asked Jimmy, pretending displeasure.

"No, I'm afraid not," Shirley giggled.

"Then you better have another one."

While they talked, Jimmy belched loudly several times. "I'm sorry," he apologized. "I've got a lot of gas in my stomach."

"Does it bother you a lot?"

"Yeah, I especially have trouble eating my favorite food," Jimmy said acting very serious about the matter.

"What's that?" asked Shirley, concerned.

"Beer." He laughed at having tricked her.

At that moment they saw Dr. Hauser making hospital rounds. Shirley greeted him: "Dr. Hauser, Jimmy spends so much time here, we're going to have to get him a job. Can't he help me in the office?"

Jimmy grinned at Dr. Hauser: "I'm going to have to get a job here to pay my medical bills."

Dr. Hauser did not say much and continued on his rounds.

Before Jimmy left, Shirley asked him about Suzie Grim. Jimmy said Suzie now worked as a TWA stewardess. "She's still a rookie, so she gets the worst assignments," he explained. "She's on reserve most of the time and never knows from one day to the next when or where she'll be flying." Jimmy explained that Suzie had accumulated eight days leave and would be visiting him soon—in fact tomorrow.

"You should marry her," Shirley suggested.

"No."

"Why not?"

"I'm too young. Maybe when I'm a little older, I'll settle down and get married."

At 4:00 A.M. Tuesday morning Suzie Grim arrived on the night flight from Indianapolis. Dana Caruthers met Suzie at the airport and drove her to the parking lot in front of Tustin Community Hospital, where Jimmy had asked his mother to leave her Cadillac so Suzie could use it. It was too early to enter the hospital, so Suzie crawled into the back seat of the Cadillac and went to sleep.

Several hours later she awoke and entered the hospital. It was 7:30 A.M., well before visiting hours at the sprawling one-floor hospital, but Suzie merely walked to Jimmy's room and went in. She spent the day with him, waiting for his release.

During that day Dr. Irving Drumm visited Jimmy in his room, the first opportunity he had to meet his new patient. Dr. Drumm, young, bespectacled, scholarly, was an oncologist, a specialist in tumors. His practice largely consisted of dealing with terminal cancer patients.

In practicing medicine Dr. Drumm attempted to extend

the lives of these terminal patients as best he could. He commiserated with them and made them as comfortable as possible. His job was eking out a few more months of life for each of his patients and lightening their burden of dying, trying to de-emphasize the feeling of terror from impending doom. He dealt with the living dead. In the field of oncology the mortality rate approximates ninety percent.

Dr. Drumm did not mention that ninety percent mortality rate when he walked into Jimmy's room. His habit was not to increase the worries harbored by his patients. He tried to let a ray of hope shine into their lives. "One reason why your abdomen has been enlarging," he explained, "is because the tumor has begun to grow again." Dr. Drumm carefully used the word "tumor," rather than the word "cancer."

"What do we do now?" asked Jimmy.

"Well, it is my opinion that further radiation treatment could prove useless."

"How come?"

"The particular metastatic tumor you now have does not respond well to radiotherapy. Besides, you have had about as much radiation as you can tolerate."

Jimmy nodded, thankful for the reprieve from the discomforting treatment, yet uncertain whether the alternative might prove even worse. He glanced at Suzie to see what her reaction might be. There was none.

Dr. Drumm continued, "We've decided on a regimen of chemotherapy. "We'll treat you with chemical drugs. We have in mind a particular program pioneered by a physician named Dr. Anderson down in Texas. He has been very successful treating patients with combined dosages of two drugs—velban and bleomycin."

"Miracle drugs?"

"There are no miracles in cancer treatment," remarked

Dr. Drumm evenly. "But this program offers some promise. It is called the VB-2 program. The chemicals will attack the tumor growing in your system and attempt to kill it. Both chemicals in combination are extremely toxic. In effect, we're trying to poison the tumor. There are risks involved and some unpleasant side effects."

"Like what?"

"You may lose all the hair on your head."

Jimmy affected a smile and turned to Suzie. "I guess you'll have to get used to the Yul Brynner look." She laughed but not too comfortably.

Dr. Drumm further cautioned that these extremely toxic drugs could lower his blood count and drop his resistance to the point where he would have difficulty fighting off other infections. Applying chemotherapy to a patient's system was very tricky, because too large a dosage may kill the patient, but too small a dosage will fail to affect the tumor. "We have to walk a very fine line," said Dr. Drumm.

"I suppose it's a little bit like the first turn at Indianapolis," offered Jimmy. "If you drive too deep into it, you crash."

Dr. Drumm looked at Jimmy and slowly nodded his head in agreement. "Precisely," he said.

Jimmy shrugged, "Well, what have I got to lose?"

Dr. Drumm outlined the treatment schedule. He would receive alternate dosages of velban and bleomycin for a period of seven days while in the hospital. Then he would be free for twenty-one days. The treatment would be repeated during two more seven-day periods, spaced out over a period of three months.

"What are my odds?"

Dr. Drumm looked down at the sheath of papers in his metal folder and, as though reading from a prepared text, said slowly, "The probability is sixty-five to seventy percent

211

that we can achieve remission." As he voiced the word "remission," Dr. Drumm glanced up and looked at Jimmy's eyes.

Jimmy, however, was staring into space. "Those are better odds than I have in a race car." The thought suddenly crossed his mind that he had uttered similar words less than a year before. Somehow, in the interim, the odds in his favor had decreased. Would he be back in the hospital a year from now, being offered still lower odds? He looked at Dr. Drumm: "Can I race?"

"Assuming we don't have any problems during treatment, I expect that you can race again."

"In time for Turkey Night? There's an important race I want to run on Thanksgiving."

"Hopefully you'll be racing by then."

"I have some appearances for Champion I need to make—"

"I don't see any problems."

"—I'm going to need to make them to help pay my hospital bills." Jimmy Caruthers already was looking down the road, seeing himself back in the seat of his race car, running at Turkey Night, maybe winning it for the first time, back on the championship car circuit, driving again at Indianapolis, maybe winning the 500. He knew that sooner or later he was going to win the big one. He hoped it could be sooner—maybe this year.

Dr. Drumm continued to reassure his patient: "In remission you will be like anybody else. There will be no tumor—or very little in the way of a tumor—to contend with. You'll feel reasonably good. If everything goes according to schedule, you can go back to racing."

Jimmy glanced at Suzie, already feeling reassured by the physician's words—or what he *thought* to be the physician's words. Dr. Drumm had carefully qualified the remarks he offered to this possibly terminal patient. There would be, at most, *very little* cancer. He would feel *reasonably* good. This would all happen *if everything goes according to schedule*. And his patient had not asked the key question concerning the meaning of the word *remission*.

Jimmy had not noticed the physician's qualifications. Instead he heard the encouraging tone of his remarks. Most encouraging was Dr. Drumm's promise that he could "go back to racing." That was the main thing that interested him.

Yet Jimmy still seemed disturbed about his swollen belly. "I can't even fit into the cockpit when I'm bloated this way," he told the doctor.

"The belly should come down."

"But what if it doesn't?"

"If worst comes to worst, we'll drain the fluid out again and you can drive."

As Dr. Drumm walked down the hospital corridor, away from Jimmy Caruthers' room, he thought that his new patient had taken the news very well, like an adult, with no tears, with no visible emotion that would have proved difficult to deal with and complicated his day.

Dr. Drumm liked that. He disliked complications in his dealings with patients. He did not enjoy working with patients whose fear of dying overwhelmed their normal emotional restraints. He much preferred working with a patient who had the attitude, aggressiveness, and desire to live which Jimmy had. He knew that he would enjoy his brief relationship with Jimmy Caruthers.

At the same time he cautioned himself not to become too involved with the young man. As he walked down the corridor away from the room containing his new patient, he knew that the stocky young man with the curly hair was named Jimmy Caruthers. He was personable, bright, much younger than his average patient. The young man was very concerned about returning to racing, and Dr.

Drumm felt a certain compassion for him in this matter and hoped that he would succeed in getting his patient back in a race car again.

But Dr. Drumm knew he must avoid identifying too closely with Jimmy Caruthers' problems. As he walked out the front door of Tustin Community Hospital and into the parking lot to climb into his car at the end of the day, to return to his wife and family, he would temporarily block all information about Jimmy Caruthers from his mind. Jimmy Caruthers would no longer be Jimmy Caruthers. He would be a patient in Room 104, someone to be returned to and seen on his next round of visits in the hospital, a young man with a tumor, a disease, a person no different from any other person with cancer.

It was the only way you could maintain your own peace of mind while dealing with the living dead. Dr. Drumm believed an oncologist could not—should not—become emotionally involved with his patients because practically none of them survived. Sooner or later, they all died, and usually it was sooner.

This was difficult for him, as a man with normal feelings of his own, to accept. It became more difficult if his patients became close friends. He recalled one small child whose death had become a tearing experience for him and, through him, for his family. This was unfair to them. He could not afford the emotional involvement of so many close friends dying week after week, so he attempted to maintain a professional policy of sympathy with noninvolvement, something not always easy to do, particularly in the case of a young man dying of cancer.

Because his patient *was* dying. Jimmy Caruthers was a terminal case. There was no question about that fact. People simply did not recover from the type of disease he had. Dr. Drumm knew that his young patient would die, and that the chemotherapy treatment he held out to him like a life line was merely a holding action, an attempt to main-

tain the quality of his patient's life at a reasonable level until the resistance to the medication recurred and his cancer
began growing again.

During their meeting he told the young man that the
odds of obtaining "remission" were sixty-five to seventy
percent; then he paused to see if the young man would ask
him what he meant by "remission." The young man did
not. His patients never did. Nobody ever asked him to
define that word—remission—perhaps because most patients try to be optimistic, and they equate the word "remission" with the word "cure"—which it is not. Or maybe
those who suspect that remission may not mean cure do
not want their fears confirmed.

Few of Dr. Drumm's patients achieved a cure. There
were no miracles for them. They merely went into holding
patterns, like airplanes constantly circling an airport in
heavy fog, but sooner or later, one way or another, they
must come down to earth. But then, every human being is
in a holding pattern and sooner or later must come down
to earth.

Dr. Drumm estimated that his patient might last one
year. Although he did not reveal that estimate, he had not
lied when he talked to the young man. He told Jimmy as
much as he wanted to know. If Jimmy had asked him for
such an estimate, he would have given it to him. But the
young man seemed more preoccupied with life than with
death. Jimmy Caruthers thought it important to return to
racing and to make some appearances, and Dr. Drumm
hoped he could give him that.

12

On Wednesday Jimmy Caruthers began a series of tests to determine what dosages of chemotherapy his body could tolerate. The first was a brain scan. He returned on Thursday for a lung scan and a bone marrow test. The latter would indicate how much his bone marrow had recovered since radiation treatment the previous spring and would suggest what ability Jimmy retained to fight infection. On Friday he had another brain scan.

Jimmy telephoned Denny Bender of Champion to cancel his scheduled appearance in Albany, but asked Bender not to shift any of his other assignments since he hoped to get back on the road between treatments and the appearances would help take his mind off his condition.

Bender was puzzled. Jimmy seemed to be talking around the subject, as though avoiding saying something. "What's your condition?" he asked.

"I've got another dose of it."

"Cancer?"

"That's the name."

"I'm sorry to hear that," said Bender, fumbling for the right words.

"Denny, don't tell anyone," pleaded Jimmy. "If you get asked, simply say I'm in the hospital undergoing tests."

"I understand."

"And don't worry. The doctors say they can cure what I've got."

Denny Bender wondered if Jimmy was telling him the truth, or if the doctors were telling Jimmy the truth. "At least I've got some good news for you," he informed Jimmy.

"I need some good news right now. What is it?"

"I checked into the insurance you carry as a member of the Champion Racing Team. You're covered."

"That's a relief," said Jimmy, and hung up.

He later told those few friends and members of his family who knew about the recurrence of his cancer that if anyone called, they should say he was merely having "tests." That was the key word—tests. He did not want people to know. He did not want others feeling sorry for him. Above all, he did not want anything said that might jeopardize his ability to get back in a race car.

Suzie and Jimmy spent most of their time between tests sitting in various waiting rooms at and around Tustin Community Hospital. On the first day Shirley Fitzpatrick appeared carrying a large bouquet of flowers. "Jimmy, these flowers are for you," she announced. The flowers had been sent by one of his friends, but arrived after he checked out of the hospital.

"I don't want any flowers," said Jimmy. "I'm not dying."

"What do you want me to do with them?"

"Give them to some old lady."

"I know a girl who's getting married this weekend," suggested Shirley.

"Yeah, perfect."

The tests proved difficult for Jimmy. During one of the tests he had to drink a large quantity of water, but experienced problems holding the water in his stomach. Despite having fluid drained from his stomach the previous Saturday, it became bloated again, almost as badly as before. He vomited the water. He had to return the following day and take the liquid into his system intravenously.

"Can't I have my stomach drained again?" he asked Dr. Hauser at this time.

"No," the surgeon replied. "The fluid in your stomach is merely a protective reaction of your body trying to coat and isolate a foreign substance—the growing tumor."

"So you can't drain it anymore?"

"If we artificially remove the fluid, the defense mechanisms of your body would automatically produce more fluids. If we continually drain your stomach, it would be too great a strain on your system."

Jimmy seemed puzzled. "I thought Dr. Drumm said the fluid could be drained to allow me back in a race car."

Dr. Hauser frowned. He did not like being caught in disagreement with another physician. "Perhaps he was talking about *after* we bring the tumor under control."

Jimmy said he understood. But when he returned to his apartment, he found it impossible to eat any food because of the fluid filling his stomach. Suzie called Dr. Hauser about this difficulty. Dr. Hauser recommended that she give him Tiger's Milk, a form of high-protein milk shake. Jimmy could not even retain that in his stomach.

On Saturday morning Doug and Dana visited La Palma to bring Jimmy some information on Laetrile, a cancer drug not available in the United States. Many desperate cancer patients had crossed the border into Mexico to buy the drug, hoping for a miracle. Jimmy thanked them, but said he did not feel desperate.

They planned a trip that afternoon to El Cajon for a California Racing Association sprint car event, driving

Don Edmunds' motor home. En route Doug told Jimmy he had arranged for them to stop and see Virginia Livingston, M.D., a cancer specialist. The father of one of Dan Gurney's mechanics worked as a physician at Dr. Livingston's clinic and arranged for an appointment for both Jimmy and his father.

Jimmy said nothing, but he was irritated that Gurney's mechanic, and even as close a friend as Don Edmunds, now knew. He did not like people making plans for him. It all seemed like a conspiracy.

When they stopped in San Diego and saw Dr. Livingston, however, she impressed him with her theories of immunotherapy. Dr. Livingston told Doug she felt certain she could help him; she seemed more reserved when talking to his son. "I'm not sure what I can do for you, Jimmy," the physician said, "although I would be willing to try."

"Well, I don't know."

"I can tell you one thing—if you decide to take chemotherapy, you'll never come out of that hospital."

Later, Jimmy and Doug discussed whether or not to go to Dr. Livingston for treatment. Jimmy decided he would not, that he would remain with the physicians already handling his case. He trusted them. At the same time he thought Dr. Livingston's immunotherapy treatments might benefit his father, whose cancer apparently was arrested. "If I were in your position, I might go to her," Jimmy advised Doug.

Doug told him, "There is absolutely no problem as far as finances."

"I know," replied Jimmy with a nod to show he did.

"We'll send you to Mexico, Switzerland, Japan," promised Doug. "We'll do whatever it takes to find a cure. Between Uncle Red and me, we have plenty of money."

"I don't want to try anything radical," Jimmy explained. "I believe in the doctors I have."

At the racetrack Jimmy encountered Rosie Rosenhof,

the announcer who interviewed him at San Bernardino. "What's new, Jimmy?" the announcer asked.

Jimmy matter-of-factly said they were still making tests and that he expected to be recovered by Turkey Night. "I'll be okay, Rosie," he said.

Rosie thought Jimmy looked weaker than when he saw him nine days earlier in San Bernardino. When Jimmy walked through the grandstands to sit down, several people he knew failed to recognize him—or pretended not to recognize him. Before the feature event started, Jimmy announced to Suzie that he no longer felt well and wanted to lie down in the motor home. She went with him and the two waited alone, not conversing, until the others finished watching the races.

The day after the trip Edmunds talked to Doug about Jimmy: "God almighty, Doug, he was a disaster!"

"He's not feeling well," Doug conceded.

"Not feeling well? Hell, he couldn't eat." Edmunds threw his hands up in despair. "I'll bet he didn't drink more than a quarter glass of milk and have a couple bites of cantaloupe. That was it for the whole day!"

"I know," responded Doug, showing his worry.

"What are we going to do with him?"

"I'm not sure there's much we can do," shrugged Doug. "Jimmy has a mind of his own."

Doug later talked to Jimmy about Dr. Livingston once more, and they discussed a book the physician wrote. "The lady has a lot of good ideas," Jimmy conceded. "Why don't you start treatments with her?"

"What about you?" Doug wanted to know.

"Hey, I don't have time to be messing around. Maybe she could cure me and maybe not, but right now I'm dealing with life or death."

Doug repeated his promise to send his son anywhere in the world for any kind of treatment. Jimmy admitted that he and Suzie had discussed that same question again and again. Suzie wanted Jimmy to consider the Sloan-Ketter-ing Clinic in New York, but he was not convinced that treatment there was superior to that available at Tustin Community Hospital.

On Monday Jimmy returned for more tests, another bone scan. Tuesday he visited Dr. Drumm in the physician's office and learned that chemotherapy would begin as soon as the results of the tests could be analyzed and the right dosages for the chemotherapy determined. Suzie remained outside in the car when Jimmy saw Dr. Drumm. She had become increasingly concerned, however, because of his inability to hold anything in his stomach. She called Dr. Hauser again, but was told not to worry. Jimmy's inability to eat was normal for his particular condition.

Suzie later telephoned Dana. "Normal?" Suzie cried. "A whole week without eating is normal?"

She felt that living with Jimmy during this period was like living with a wounded cobra. He was continually nauseated, always uncomfortable, and so edgy that he did not want anyone near him. Once while he was sitting in a bean-bag chair in the living room of their apartment, Suzie moved to the chair, putting her arm around his shoulder. He winced. "That hurts," he said, and immediately felt sorry for saying it. He knew the comment wounded her. "I shouldn't have said that," he apologized.

"I know you don't feel well." She tried to soothe him.

"I'll be better soon."

"I know you will." She smiled, but it was a weak smile.

"Maybe when I do, we can get married. How would you like to be a Christmas bride?"

Suzie wanted to hear those words, but she was not certain she wanted to hear them at that moment.

"You're just saying that because you know I want to hear it."

"No, I'm not," Jimmy insisted. "I mean it."

"It would make a nice Christmas present. Even better than Indian jewelry."

"You don't like what I gave you last Christmas?" probed Jimmy, suddenly reverting to his old, teasing self.

Suzie smiled, aware that Jimmy was teasing her. But her face grew serious again.

"I didn't say that," she said quietly.

Suzie's eight-day leave ended on Tuesday and Jimmy drove her to the airport, knowing she would make a big scene. It was not because he had cancer; Suzie always made big scenes at airports. She never cried at racetracks; only at airports. Even if they planned only a three-day separation, she often burst into tears. But after he kissed her good-bye and she started to go down the ramp, she turned and smiled. "I'll see you real soon."

Jimmy smiled, too. "Babe, I'm really proud of you."

His comment puzzled her.

"Why is that?"

"You're not crying."

"I know," she whispered softly.

"Thanks," he said, and from the look in his eyes she could tell he really meant it.

"Jimmy, I'm proud of you, too," said Suzie. Then she was gone, down the ramp and into the airplane.

Jimmy drove back to the La Palma apartment alone. Later that evening Dana called to see how he was doing. "Well, we made it through the big airport scene without any tears."

"You mean Suzie didn't cry?" asked Dana.

"No," said Jimmy. "I didn't cry."

But after he hung up the telephone, he realized that he was now crying. He wanted to call Suzie as soon as she landed in Chicago and tell her to catch the next plane back. He did not do so.

Suzie returned to her job the next day, staying in the apartment near O'Hare field she shared with the two other airline stewardesses. On Wednesday she flew to New York on a turnaround, returning the same day. Thursday she flew to Philadelphia on a layover, staying overnight and flying back to Chicago on Friday. Saturday she had a trip to Las Vegas. Every night she called Jimmy to ask how he felt. He said he was feeling okay, that he would be beginning chemotherapy soon, that everything was all right, that she should not worry.

Jimmy remained alone in the La Palma apartment now. Gene Romero was off in the Midwest trying to obtain sponsorship from Harley-Davidson for the next year's racing season. Dana stopped by on Wednesday to see Jimmy and thought he looked much weaker. It was almost as though he had pumped himself up to appear as strong as possible before Suzie's departure, then deflated like a balloon once she left. He lay around the apartment doing nothing, waiting for something to happen, but not knowing what it might be.

Dana told Jimmy she thought he should be in the hospital, but he insisted he would be going there in a few days. She left, unable to get him to eat, unable to convince him to go where he at least could receive nourishment intravenously. Later she and Doug discussed what to do about getting Jimmy out of the apartment. Doug felt he could not tell Jimmy to move; that, if anything, it would inspire his son to do exactly the opposite. He finally decided to call his former wife, Jimmy's mother, to see if she would intervene.

But when he called her, La Vey Caruthers showed little interest in talking to Doug—about anything. She could not overcome the bitterness she felt toward Doug since his marriage to a younger woman, even though that marriage occurred a dozen years after their divorce. She said that Jimmy was all right, that he went to see Dr. Drumm that day, that the doctors were waiting for the drugs to arrive for the chemotherapy treatments. Doug argued that Jimmy should go to the hospital immediately, so he could at

least receive some care to prevent his strength and re-
serves from being further depleted. His ex-wife disagreed.
"The boy's dying!" Doug shouted. "What kind of people
are we that we can't overcome our own differences at a
time like this?" But she would not discuss the subject further. She said Jimmy would be all right. Doug slammed
down the telephone, furious, in tears. "I just can't get
through to that woman!"

Jimmy planned to spend the day with his young son on
Thursday, but called his mother the next morning to say
he could not come. That day Dana returned to see Jimmy
again, this time accompanied by Bobby Capels, wife of
Jimmy's mechanic. They knocked on the door, and Jimmy
shouted from inside to come in. The door was unlocked.

He lay on the couch in his shorts. Dana was stunned at
how much weaker he looked. His stomach was so bloated,
she told Doug later, that he looked like a woman nine
months pregnant. She went into the bedroom, where she
found, and was nauseated by, a glass containing brownish
fluid. Jimmy had been spitting up the fluid.

After the visit Dana talked to Doug about his son's condition. She was clearly angry. "He's so much worse than
yesterday that you wouldn't believe it."

"He's that bad?" sighed Doug, not wanting to hear it.

"And those damn doctors. They won't do anything to
get him out of there!" Dana showed she was furious.

"They're busy."

"That's what I mean!" snapped Dana.

"I don't know what to do," admitted Doug nervously,
not knowing what to do. If it was a broken car, he could fix
it. But broken humans were out of his field.

"I don't know what to do either, but we're going to get
him into that hospital if I have to go over there with a gun
in my hands!"

"At this point," said Doug evenly, "I'm not sure Jimmy
would be frightened by a gun."

Doug called his brother and asked if he would go over to

224

Jimmy's apartment and convince him to check into the hospital immediately. Uncle Red seemed to feel it was unnecessary. His wife, Virginia, had been keeping in touch through Jimmy's mother, and she said he was doing all right. Doug, however, insisted that Red go over and talk to him. Red promised he would do so. Ten minutes later the telephone rang. It was Red. He said he talked to Jimmy on the telephone and his nephew said he was feeling all right. "Bullshit, Red!" screamed Doug. "The kid's lying to you!" But Uncle Red did not feel there was much he could do.

"Maybe we could get Johnny Capels to see him," Dana finally suggested. "His wife, Bobby, was over there with me and saw how bad Jimmy is."

When Doug called Johnny Capels, the mechanic said he would visit Jimmy and one way or another get him into the hospital.

But when Capels went to Jimmy's apartment that night and rang the bell, nobody answered. He rang again; still nobody answered. Capels began to worry. He knew Jimmy was home; he could see his car parked in the parking lot. He tried the door. It was unlocked.

The apartment was dark. "Jimmy, are you there?" No answer. Capels' worries increased. "Jimmy!" he shouted again. Still no answer.

Capels thought he heard the sound of running water. "Jimmy!" He turned on the light and walked into the living room. The sound of running water came from the corridor leading to the bedrooms at the far end of the apartment. Capels walked down the corridor as far as the bathroom door. He opened it, and a flood of steam engulfed him. Inside, sitting in the bathtub, with the shower playing on his distended stomach, was Jimmy Caruthers. He stared up at his mechanic, but said nothing.

"What the hell are you doing?" asked Capels.

"The hot water sometimes relieves the pain in my back," Jimmy explained.

"You belong in a hospital."

"Not yet."

Capels' Greek temper exploded. "You disappoint me, Jimmy. I thought you were a fighter, but you're nothing but a goddam sissy! What are you doing, just lying here dying?"

"I'm not dying."

"You've given up!" screamed Capels. "Goddam you, Caruthers, you've given up! You're not even trying, goddam you!"

Jimmy just stared up at him.

Capels continued, "You need to be in a hospital. You need to be fed intravenously. You need to have your stomach tapped. You need to be getting your strength back so you can start chemotherapy. And what are you doing? You're just lying here in the bathtub, resisting every effort on the part of anybody to help you."

"Don't worry," Jimmy finally said. "Everything will be fine by the first of the year."

"What does that mean?"

Jimmy finally allowed Capels to lift him out of the bathtub and turn off the water. He said he wanted to go to bed now. The telephone rang, and it was Suzie calling from Philadelphia. "Yeah, I'm feeling fine," Jimmy told her. "Much better."

When he hung up the receiver, Capels told Jimmy, "You're even lying to Suzie. Don't you know what's happening to you?"

"I know."

"Well, what do you plan to do about it?"

Jimmy stared at his mechanic for what seemed like a very long time. He finally said, "I think I'm ready to go into the hospital."

On Friday morning Jimmy called Dr. Drumm's office and learned that the chemotherapy could begin the next day. His mother came to drive him to the hospital. Kay

Smith, head nurse on the pediatrics ward, looked up from her desk and saw Jimmy Caruthers standing before her at three o'clock that afternoon. She remembered him from the previous year.

Although most patients in the pediatrics ward were young children, the hospital had four rooms near the entrance to the ward usually occupied by young adults, aged twenty to thirty. Nurse Smith assigned him to one of these rooms, at Dr. Hauser's request, because it would be easier to isolate him from the rest of the hospital population. Because of the weakening effect of the drugs on his resistance, it was important to keep him free from infection.

The pediatrics ward at Tustin Community Hospital was particularly warm and cheery, all yellows and golds, with airplanes, pink rhinos, and tin soldiers decorating the corridor walls. The design on the wallpaper in Jimmy's room consisted of graffiti and cartoons illustrating the graffiti— Making the scene, Chicks, Dig, Up tight, Heavy, Cool it, Taking a trip.

Jimmy Caruthers felt in no mood to enjoy the messages on his walls. He was sick, and weak, and hungry, having had very little nourishment since leaving the hospital ten days before. "Can you get me something to eat?" he asked Nurse Smith after he changed into his hospital gown.

"I'll contact your doctor," she promised. When she returned to the nursing station, she telephoned Dr. Hauser, who ordered a food tray for Jimmy. He ate, but vomited almost immediately. Nurse Smith felt Jimmy looked disappointed, very sad, as though he had failed.

When Dr. Hauser first saw Jimmy in the hospital, he felt the odds against him looked grim. Because of his swollen stomach, Jimmy was having difficulty breathing. To Dr. Hauser, Jimmy looked like he was going out in a day or two.

Although technically Jimmy was now Dr. Drumm's patient, Dr. Hauser, who was present more frequently in the hospital, continued to manage Jimmy's day-to-day problems, including his nausea. On Saturday he ordered a hyperalimentation tap, an intravenous feeding through the carotid artery in his neck. He also drained the fluid from Jimmy's stomach. Jimmy's back still hurt him, and with the tap, he had to keep his head still, which added to his discomfort. Even the back rubs the nurses gave him seemed only partially to cure his distress, but with his stomach drained and with the intravenous feedings begun, his strength gradually returned.

Dr. Drumm began chemotherapy that day, utilizing the VB-2 treatment, consisting of two doses each of the drugs velban and bleomycin spaced out over a period of seven days. Jimmy Caruthers was only the sixth patient under Dr. Drumm's care to be given the VB-2 treatment.

The nurses also considered Jimmy an easy patient. Mary Hill, one of the floor nurses, noticed that whenever she did some favor for Jimmy, no matter how insignificant, like raising his bed or fluffing his pillow, he always thanked her. She came from Scotland, knew nothing about American auto racing, and never realized that Jimmy Caruthers raced in something called an "Indy 500"—whatever that was—until she heard some of the other floor personnel talking about it.

Randy de Runtz, another nurse, liked Jimmy because he was pleasant to deal with. In addition, Dr. Hauser seemed more personally involved in Jimmy's case than with many of his other patients, and when he came in to examine Jimmy's charts and see him, he shared his medical information with the nursing staff. Jimmy also seemed somewhat special because of his being one of only a handful of adults in a ward devoted mostly to children.

As Jimmy's strength gradually returned, he began to worry again about getting back in his race car. He questioned both Dr. Drumm and Dr. Hauser about his condition. "How soon will I be able to get out of the hospital?" he asked the former one day.

"We should be finished with the first phase of chemotherapy by next Saturday," Dr. Drumm replied. "If everything goes well, you'll be out of the hospital on Sunday."

"But can I race?"

"Hopefully, you will be able to race."

"You're positive?"

"Don't worry, Jimmy. If the treatment progresses the way we expect, we'll get you back on the racetrack."

Jimmy hoped Dr. Drumm told him the truth, but to further assure himself he called Dave Clutter in Indianapolis. They talked about the chemotherapy and the chances of its successfully containing the tumor. "What are my chances?" asked Jimmy bluntly.

"I don't know," admitted Dr. Clutter.

"What do you mean, you don't know? You're a doctor, aren't you?"

"Well, if you had called me last winter and asked me what your chances were, I would have said you never would have raced last summer."

"I fooled everybody once. I'll fool them again," said Jimmy. He made Dr. Clutter promise not to talk to anybody about his condition, especially their friends. Dr. Clutter hung up, feeling Jimmy was being dishonest with him for the first time, both in minimizing how sick he was and in telling him not to talk to others. He *had* been talking to others, and they said Jimmy was telling them the same thing.

Dr. Clutter felt it extremely unlikely that Jimmy could return to racing after cancer had spread to another part of his body. He called Dr. Hauser to obtain more detailed information on the treatment because, after talking to Jimmy, he was unclear as to what was going on. Dr. Hauser told Dr. Clutter he was optimistic, that he believed the drugs would work.

After his conversation with Dr. Hauser, Dr. Clutter felt better about Jimmy's chances.

On Sunday Larry Griffith, the mechanic for the Pizza Hut dirt car, called Jimmy's apartment in La Palma. He and owner George Middleton, anticipating the 1976 racing season, wanted to talk to Jimmy about his plans. Gene Romero, just returned from his Midwest trip, answered the phone. Burritto said his roommate was back in the hospital, but only "to get some checks."

Griffith, surprised and worried, called the hospital and talked to the driver. "Do you want to race for us again?"

"You bet I do," Jimmy responded.

As defending USAC champion, Jimmy earned the right to race the following season with a number one on his car, instead of the number fifty-five, which he used in 1974. "Do you want to run a number one, or shall we keep the fifty-five?" asked Larry.

"Larry, I want you to paint the biggest goddam one that you can get on that thing!"

"You're sure?"

"We won it; we're going to run it."

As the chemotherapy treatments continued, either Dr. Drumm or his partner saw Jimmy every day. "Are we on schedule?" Jimmy kept asking.

"We're on schedule."

"I've got to get out of here," Jimmy kept insisting. "I've got commitments."

Bev Pomeroy, one of the floor nurses, talked to him one day about his racing. She read in the paper recently about some big race through the streets of Long Beach and wondered if Jimmy raced in it. He said no, but he had gone over to watch. "Doesn't it scare you when you race?" she asked.

Jimmy said he was not scared.

"But don't you worry," she probed, "that you might not be able to finish the race, that you might crash?"

Jimmy said it did not worry him and that if you want to

succeed in auto racing, you have to accept the possibility of your own death in a race car. If this bothers you, you simply climb out of the race car and do something else. He knew a lot of drivers who did just that. But it did not bother him. "The thing I really enjoy about racing is going fast," he told her.

They talked about other drivers that he knew—Lee Kunzman, Gary Bettenhausen, Billy Vukovich—but the names meant nothing to her. They discussed the type of cars he raced—championship cars, midget cars, dirt cars—but all it did was puzzle her. She was astounded by the amount of money it cost to build the cars that raced at Indianapolis—$100,000 in some cases. "My goodness," said Nurse Pomeroy. "That's a lot of money."

"It's going to cost a lot of money to get out of this hospital, too," Jimmy grimaced.

On Tuesday Jimmy Caruthers felt better than he had in several weeks. When Dr. Hauser saw him that day, he felt encouraged. "It looks as though the chemotherapy is succeeding," he told one of the nurses.

Among the visitors that day was Uncle Red. Jimmy asked Uncle Red if he could find some way to get his pickup truck transported from Indianapolis to the West Coast. "I'm getting out on Sunday and I'd like to work on it," said Jimmy. Uncle Red promised he would call a mutual friend in Indianapolis and see what he could arrange.

Uncle Red later talked to his brother. "Doug, the boy's going to be all right."

Burritto also stopped by the hospital that afternoon. The motorcycle racer planned a week's vacation with his girl friend, Nancy, but remained in town, worried about his roommate's condition. Jimmy joked and laughed with him, and when one of the nurses came in, he introduced her, saying to Burritto, "This is my nurse when you're not around."

Burritto thought Jimmy looked great. He decided to

leave that day on his vacation and told Jimmy he planned to head on up to Reno. "Hey, good buddy, I'll keep you posted," said Burritto, and left.

Jimmy seemed able, finally, to hold food in his stomach. During the day Nurse Randy de Runtz brought him milk shakes on three occasions. He drank every one. That night Nurse Kay Smith walked into his room and found him watching the cartoon show "Speed Racer" on television. "That's one of my favorite shows," she said. "I have a four-year-old boy and I like to watch it with him."

"I have a four-year-old, too," said Jimmy. "We sometimes watch it together." He discovered her son was named Jim, too, not after a race driver, however. They talked briefly about the TV show and their children. It was the only time she recalled talking either about racing or his personal life with Jimmy Caruthers.

She did notice the improvement in his sense of humor. As she was leaving, her skirt got caught on his side rail. "Why does this always happen in your room?"

He smiled at her. "Because you want it to happen."

On Wednesday morning, when Nurse Mary Hill came in to see him, she found Jimmy coming out of the bathroom. He said, "I don't feel so good today."

She offered him breakfast, but he said he did not want to eat. "Would you at least take some orange juice?"

"Just leave it."

Later that day Nurse Bev Pomeroy told Jimmy that Suzie Grim was on the telephone and wanted to talk to him. Suzie was on a turnaround flight from Chicago to Las Vegas and back to Chicago. She called Jimmy during the brief Las Vegas layover. Jimmy seemed reluctant to talk to his girl friend, worrying that if Suzie learned he was feeling bad again, she might leave her job and come back to California. She was low in seniority and still on probation, and he feared TWA might fire her for excessive absences. He wanted her to keep her stewardess job, and he did not want her sitting around the hospital with him sick. "Tell her the doctor is here and I can't talk now," said Jimmy.

Nurse Pomeroy worried that Jimmy might be hiding his condition from his girl friend. She also noticed that there seemed to be a division between different family groups that visited him. She did not understand what the division was, or why it was, but she noticed that some did not get along well with others. She asked Jimmy if Suzie was being kept informed about his medical progress.

"Yeah," said Jimmy. "My mom calls her every day."

That afternoon Johnny Parsons, Jr., flew in from Palm Springs following an appearance for Champion. He stopped by the hospital, accompanied by motorcycle racer Chuck Palmgran of Santa Ana. Parsons thought his friend looked dejected. He was not in the room for more than a few minutes when one of the nurses, Kay Smith, asked him to leave. "No visitors allowed other than the immediate family," she said.

The next morning Parsons returned and stood outside Jimmy's door just to see him. Jimmy's mother, who spent most of her days at the hospital, sat inside with her son. Jimmy looked weak, but he got out of bed and waved. Parsons found it hard to carry on a conversation. Finally, he just said, "Hurry up and get out of here."

Dana appeared that afternoon and asked Jimmy how he felt. "I'd love to get out of bed," he said. "My back is killing me." Dana and the nurse carried each of the two intravenous poles and helped walk him from one side of the bed to the other. He sat down in a chair. Dana obtained some cream from the nurse and began rubbing his back. "God," said Jimmy. "You are the worst back-rubber in the world!"

"Do you want me to call Suzie for you or anything?"

"No, my mom keeps her informed. It gives Mom something to do."

After Dana returned home, Suzie called from Chicago. She was crying. She had been trying to get through to Jimmy on the telephone for three days without success. She could not get information from the hospital. "What is happening out there?" she wanted to know.

"Isn't Jimmy's mom keeping you informed?" questioned Dana. "He said she was."

"I never heard from her once."

Suzie seemed less concerned about that than she was about Jimmy's condition. "How is he?"

"He seemed weaker yesterday and today," Dana admitted.

"Weaker?"

"But apparently that's to be expected with the drugs he's taking. You remember how bad he felt last winter during those cobalt treatments. Everybody seems hopeful that the drugs will arrest the cancer."

"Should I come out there?"

"I don't know."

"I could ask for a leave from my job and come to California."

Dana thought for a while, then told her, "Your being a stewardess means a lot to Jimmy, and I don't think he would want you doing anything that might jeopardize your job."

On Friday morning Dana telephoned Jimmy and he sounded cheerful. "Guess what happened to me this morning?"

"What?"

"The doctors finally let me take a bath. You won't have to stand upwind of me anymore."

"Jimmy, I talked to Suzie on the telephone last night. She said your mother hasn't been calling her."

"Oh no," said Jimmy. He thought his mother had been calling her regularly. Somehow Jimmy always overlooked, or failed to recognize, the antagonism that his mother felt toward Suzie Grim because of their lack of a marriage license.

That afternoon Doug and Dana visited the hospital. Jimmy seemed groggy. Dana noticed he could hardly hold his head up or keep his eyes open. He seemed to doze off several times. Finally they got up, and Dana patted him on the shoulder. "We're going to go now." She put her hand in his.

He squeezed it very lightly. "Thanks for coming, you guys."

Shirley Fitzpatrick kept track of Jimmy's treatment from a distance by asking the pediatric nurses she met in the cafeteria about him, or by talking to his family in the waiting room. On Friday she expected Jimmy to appear for an X-ray, but the floor nurses sent word he was too sick to come to the X-ray room. One of the technicians wheeled a portable machine to his room. Shirley decided to accompany him.

Jimmy seemed happy to see her, but complained of nausea. She asked him if he was eating. He shook his head. One of the floor nurses came into the room, so Shirley started to leave. Jimmy began, "Shirley—"

She turned around, but Jimmy could not even finish the statement. "I'll be back," she promised him.

Later, she returned to his room and found him asleep.

Dr. Drumm, meanwhile, was worried. Jimmy Caruthers no longer seemed to respond well to the drugs. On Tuesday, when his strength temporarily returned, his system seemed to be tolerating the treatment. Dr. Drumm was pleased. Then his patient slid downhill. On Friday Jimmy's condition deteriorated to the point where Dr. Drumm decided to halt the chemotherapy two days ahead of schedule.

Jimmy had developed an infection—grand malinginasepsis—caused by a category of bacteria common to most human beings. Organisms grow in the bowels. An individual with normal resistance easily copes with these germs. But Jimmy Caruthers no longer possessed normal resistance. As a result, organisms began to spread into his bloodstream.

When Dr. Drumm discovered the infection, he prescribed antibiotics to stem the spread of the organisms through Jimmy's system. But antibiotics serve, at best, as temporary defenses capable of staving off the invasion of marauding germs only until the body's normal immunal mechanism can recover. The problem was that Jimmy's immunity was so overwhelmed by doses of radiation and chemotherapy to control his cancer, and his body was so debilitated by his advancing disease, that his resistance was very feeble.

Jimmy had been bombarded by radiology. His system was saturated with chemotherapy. Then the bugs start growing within him like they would on a piece of raw meat sitting on a hot sidewalk. There was no resistance—even with antibiotics. Antibiotics can tip the scales in favor of the host, but if the host has no resistance, you can tip them all you want. Nothing happens because eventually the organisms become resistant to the antibiotics and they continue to grow. They were growing now within Jimmy Caruthers.

When the antibiotics failed to halt the growing infection, Dr. Drumm realized he had lost his battle to control the cancer through chemotherapy, and to buy Jimmy some additional time, to get him back into a race car. He was a realist, and he knew he had failed. The drugs had failed. He had not expected them to do so, but it happened. A series of biochemical events had been set in motion that would lead to shock and eventually to death. Jimmy Caruthers was as good as dead, and Dr. Irving Drumm knew it. His patient was—in the word that Jimmy used after seeing his brother, Danny, run into the wall—"junk!" There was no more he could do to save him. Any further efforts on his part to continue treatment, he thought, might simply worsen Jimmy's suffering.

He did not tell Jimmy Caruthers he was dying. He did not offer this opinion to any of the nurses attending him. He did not share his views with any of the other physicians in the hospital—including Dr. Roger G. Hauser, who, despite Jimmy's sinking condition, felt that he still could save his patient's life.

13

One of the unwritten rules for physicians, nurses, and others who work in hospitals is not to become emotionally involved in the lives of their patients. They need to treat those patients with sympathy, with patience, and even with tenderness, yet have the ability to turn off their emotions when they walk out the hospital door at the end of work hours. They understand that they should not carry hospital problems home to their families. So you often hear physicians, in private conferences with their colleagues, referring to patients as the hysterectomy in Room 174, the pneumonia in Room 127, the cardiac in Room 114. They often talk of their patients as diseases to treat rather than as individuals with names, who might have wives, children, and personal problems of their own. Physicians treat and cure diseases rather than people, because physicians—as well as nurses and others who work in hospitals—have enough problems of their own without taking on the problems of the hundreds of others with whom they come in contact.

Yet on certain occasions the hospital personnel find themselves drawn to a patient who becomes an individual rather than merely a disease. Physical therapist Paul Pursell stopped by Jimmy Caruthers' room Saturday morning, talked briefly with him from the corridor, then left because he saw Jimmy did not feel well. Pursell, who rarely visited that area of the hospital, had gone to Jimmy's room because of his concern for him. Almost against his will he had become involved. He noticed others had become involved. He heard them talking about Jimmy during coffee breaks in the cafeteria, exchanging information while passing in the hall.

This was unusual. Pursell could recall only three or four occasions in the four years he worked at Tustin Community Hospital when the hospital personnel became attached to a particular patient. Usually it was someone like a local police officer, or a fireman, or maybe a young child who attracts that sort of attention. He felt it was unprofessional and undesirable to get wrapped up in someone else's life. He noticed that when it happened to one person in the hospital, usually everyone became affected.

It happened to the personnel of Tustin Community Hospital in the case of Jimmy Caruthers. Partly it was because he drove at Indianapolis and carried a certain fame with him. But that did not entirely explain the involvement, since few people showed great interest in the sport of auto racing, and celebrities were fairly common at the hospital. Partly it was because of his youth—that at the age of thirty he was dying of cancer. So the young employees of the hospital could relate to his fight for life. But people fight for life continuously in any hospital, and this is one of the main reasons for the effort to be impersonal. Mostly it seemed to be because Dr. Roger Hauser became emotionally attached to Jimmy Caruthers. Even Dr. Drumm noticed that his colleague found it difficult to release the emotional hold his patient had on him.

Because Dr. Hauser, a very popular physician among the hospital staff, became emotionally involved with Jimmy's struggle, he infected others with his concern, and they, too, became involved. Paul Pursell considered that in one sense unfortunate because it tended to make those who were supposed to be realistic unrealistic.

On Saturday morning Nurse Mary Hill walked into Jimmy's room and saw a look on his face she had not seen before. It was a look of hopelessness. It surprised her because she felt he had looked good the day before. Perspiring, he seemed to have difficulty breathing. He was propped up in bed, so she immediately rolled the bed down and took his temperature and blood pressure. Not liking what she saw, Nurse Hill called Dr. Hauser and told him Jimmy's sickness seemed to have turned into another stage.

Dr. Hauser arrived soon after and determined that, in addition to his other medical complications, Jimmy had developed pneumonia. Both lungs were beginning to fill with mucus secretions, a form of pus which, if not halted, eventually could cause him to drown in his own secretions. Dr. Hauser prescribed additional antibiotics to counteract the pneumonia, and for a few hours Jimmy stabilized and looked as though he might recover.

The nurses tried their best to comfort him, giving Jimmy rubs to relieve his still aching back. He asked if he could have a bath, hoping to relax, but it did not help.

At about three in the afternoon Nurse Kay Smith walked into Jimmy's room. She found him sitting in his chair, half-collapsed to one side, his head resting on the bed. He still had difficulty breathing. She thought he looked terrified—as though he knew something bad was happening to him, but found himself unable to do anything to avert it. One of the greatest fears of race drivers, when they drive at speeds of two hundred miles per hour on tracks like the Indianapolis Motor Speedway, is losing control. Yet most race drivers are optimists and believe that even if they temporarily lose control, and their race car slides up through the "gray stuff" headed toward the wall, they will be able to regain control and avert disaster because of their tremendous driving skills. It is an illusion, and drivers die believing this illusion, thinking that through mastery of their art they can save themselves. Jimmy not only had lost control, but he began to lose all his illusions about his ability to save it. Now all he possessed was hope that Dr. Hauser could pull him out of the wreckage and still save his life.

Nurse Bev Pomeroy tried that afternoon to comfort Jimmy, but she found that he had increased difficulty breathing. His temperature continued to rise. His body actually was red. In the late afternoon Kay Smith called Dr. Hauser, who came over and tried additional treatments, but nothing seemed to work.

Jimmy Caruthers slipped into still another stage. At six o'clock late that afternoon Dr. Hauser decided to shift his patient to an area where he could receive more attention. "I think we better move him to the ICU," he instructed Nurse Kay Smith, referring to the hospital's intensive care unit.

"It's that bad?" asked the nurse.

"I didn't say it was bad," snapped Dr. Hauser, frustrated at his own inability to work a miracle with his patient.

The orderlies came in to move Jimmy Caruthers. Nurse Smith leaned over his bed. "Jimmy, we're going to move you into a different area of the hospital."

Jimmy looked up at her but said nothing. His eyes darted back and forth from her to the orderlies now starting to move his bed. He still did not say anything. He felt too weak to talk. Besides, he could think of nothing to say.

They wheeled him out of his room with the funny sayings on the wallpaper and into the corridor. After he disappeared through the double doors that led out of the pediatric unit, Kay Smith went back to a room near the nurse's station where nobody could see her. She started to cry. She felt she would never see Jimmy Caruthers again.

As he passed along the corridor connecting the pediatrics unit on one side of the hospital building with the intensive care unit on the other, Jimmy Caruthers had the sensation of having traveled this route once before. The wheels of his bed moving along the floor of the hallway made only a slightly perceptible hum. The wall paintings of flowers and landscapes and ocean scenes seemed to form a blur beside him. Then suddenly they were not paintings but people, thousands of people on each side of the main straightaway at Indianapolis. The hum of hospital bed wheels became the scream of an engine at his back, behind him, pushing him forward faster and faster. Although he could not hear them over the roar of the accelerating engine, he knew that the people on each side were shouting his name, cheering for him to succeed, pulling for his victory. He was going to win the Big One. Before it was all over, he would be cruising into victory lane at the Indianapolis Motor Speedway, one of the immortals who had won the 500 and whose name would be remembered forever whenever race fans met.

He had this feeling as the orderlies pushed his bed down the corridor at Tustin Community Hospital, but suddenly reality dawned on him. Fate had decreed that it would not happen that way. He was hurtling down the straightaway at ever-increasing speeds, aimed at the first turn, but Jimmy knew when he reached the corner he would be unable to turn the wheel. He had lost control.

The intensive care unit at Tustin Community Hospital had been completely modernized within the past year. It contained the most advanced equipment for measuring a patient's condition. It was a marvel of modern medical science, and had Jimmy Caruthers been in condition to observe it objectively, he would have been fascinated by how efficiently it functioned on a mechanical level.

He now lay in bed in one of a number of individual cubicles next to a large control room. On his right wrist was attached a central venous pressure line and a femoral line that reached into his heart. The lines were connected to a console in the main control room where a single nurse, by examining the monitors before her, could watch his every heartbeat and determine even the change in pressure in different parts of his heart. The monitor fed through a computer which had been programmed to sound an alarm should any drastic change occur in his pulse rate, either higher or lower. At the same moment it triggered an automatic printout sheet showing electrocardiogram traces.

Those were only the attachments to one arm. Additional intravenous lines were attached to various other parts of his body—his wrists, his ankles. A rectal probe monitored his body temperature. At various times he was fed tevothet, a drug that raises one's blood pressure; dopamene, another drug that did the same; and a solution of dextrose and water for nourishment. A single nurse remained in his cubicle, giving him full-time attention, making urine tests every hour, directly monitoring the equipment, doing everything possible to keep her patient alive until either he rallied and fought off the bacteriological organisms trying to consume him, or failed. Unlike the nurses who cared for Jimmy in the pediatrics ward, however, she did not know him as an individual. She was too busy monitoring his systems to think of him as such; she knew him only as a very sick man. Months later she would not even remember having cared for him.

The care Jimmy Caruthers received resembled, in many ways, the care he was accustomed to receiving when he raced at Indianapolis. Being attached to the ICU monitor was similar to sliding into the cockpit of his race car with its blowers, fuel tubes, and hydraulic lines. Instead of a chief mechanic, he had a head nurse. His fate depended on the machine, but also upon himself.

Soon after Jimmy arrived in the intensive care unit, technician Joe Aldenhifer arrived with a portable X-ray machine. He attempted to work swiftly, causing as little discomfort to his patient as possible, yet getting a clear picture to aid diagnosis. When Dr. Hauser examined the negative, however, it displeased him. "That's a terrible X-ray," the surgeon said.

"It's the best we can do," explained Joe. One of the duty nurses seemed surprised by Dr. Hauser's outburst. He rarely reacted so angrily and usually showed more consideration for the feelings of those around him. The nurse decided that maybe he was tired and knew he was facing a losing battle.

When Aldenhifer wheeled his portable machine out of the ICU and headed back to his department, he tried not to look at the small group of people waiting in the row of chairs immediately around the corner. He noticed them when he passed on his way into the ICU and knew they were looking at him suspiciously, wondering why he had been called. Now that he was leaving he knew, again, they would look at him, still wondering, examining his face for any hint, or sign, as to what was happening to the patient inside. He stared straight ahead as he wheeled the portable machine down the corridor, not wanting to have to deal with them.

Among those waiting was Jimmy's mother. She was accompanied by Uncle Red and Aunt Virginia. After the nurses took his nephew to ICU, Uncle Red telephoned his brother, who had gone home after being at the hospital most of the day. Doug said he would return immediately.

Suzie Grim had flown another Las Vegas turnaround on Friday. Saturday she took an overnight to Pittsburgh. Doug telephoned Suzie at her motel in that city. "Jimmy's not doing too well," he told her. "He's in intensive care."

"How serious is it?" she asked.

"I don't know, but I think it's pretty bad."

After Doug hung up, Suzie debated what to do. Her immediate instinct was to climb on the first plane for Los Angeles to be with Jimmy. But as a new stewardess she worried the airline might question any sudden departure. TWA might not understand the closeness of her relationship with a man to whom she was not married. She decided to contact Dr. Hauser for further information, and located him still at the hospital. "I think you should get on the next plane," Dr. Hauser advised. "Your presence might help give him the extra strength he needs to get through the current situation."

Unfortunately, the next plane for Los Angeles did not leave until 8:45 the next morning.

The friends and family of Jimmy Caruthers remained waiting in the lobby until 4:00 A.M., when Dr. Hauser came out of the ICU and said he thought Jimmy's condition had stabilized, and that he planned to go home and get some sleep.

Four hours later the family returned to continue their vigil. Hospital regulations permitted a single person to see an ICU patient—once an hour and only for one minute. This individual had to don surgically sterile disposable clothes before gaining entry. Jimmy's mother informed her former husband that she would handle all the visits. Doug thought he would feel uncomfortable anyway seeing his son all trussed up with wires and tubes; so he offered no objection.

During the night Dr. Hauser performed a tracheotomy on Jimmy's throat to permit him to breathe more easily. With the tube in his throat he had difficulty speaking. The nurse gave him a plastic scratch pad so he could write notes to the doctor, but Jimmy had little to say. When Dr. Hauser came in to treat him, he talked with Jimmy, offered him words of encouragement, and kidded him. Jimmy smiled at him. Dr. Hauser thought at least Jimmy was holding his own.

In Philadelphia Suzie rose early and took the limousine from her hotel to the airport to catch the 8:45 flight to Los Angeles. All things considered, she had slept well the night before. She was worried that Jimmy had apparently become more sick since she last saw him. But at the same time she was relieved at finally being able to do something. At least in California she no longer would need to rely on the word of others as to Jimmy's condition.

As the jet airplane carrying her rose above the thick layer of clouds covering the East Coast and into the blue sky above, she leaned back in her seat and relaxed. She thought back about all the happy times she and Jimmy had had together. She also thought back to the sad times—the time at Pocono when he crashed and they learned his ankle was broken. But that had turned out all right. Dr. Callaghan had put the pin in his ankle and he was back in a race car within the next month. Then there was last winter, when Jimmy first learned he had cancer and thought he might never race again. He had been sick then, his body drained from the cobalt treatments. He overcame that problem with the help of Dr. Hauser and returned to racing. She felt that this latest condition was simply one more episode in Jimmy's medical history. The doctors once more would cure him so he could go racing again, and she could be with him at the races.

Suzie looked forward to seeing Jimmy and watching over his recovery. Maybe, when Jimmy would get out of the hospital this time, she could get a leave of absence and return to California to care for him. He had talked about getting married at Christmas. If they did so, maybe the airline would grant the leave without penalty.

She began to think ahead past Jimmy's recovery to the next season, when she would be more free to be with him. She looked forward to Indianapolis next May, being with their friends, being part of the greatest spectacle in auto racing again.

At 1:00 that afternoon Suzie arrived from the airport at Tustin Community Hospital at the same moment that Dr. Hauser stepped out of the intensive care unit. His face lit up and he brought her immediately into the room to see Jimmy. All of the attachments and equipment stunned her momentarily. She stood there for a moment, not knowing what to do or what to say. Was he really this sick? Jimmy seemed barely conscious. Suzie turned to Dr. Hauser: "I don't think he knows I'm here." As soon as she said that, Jimmy nodded his head.

She placed her hand on the bed near his. He reached over, picked up her hand, and placed it on his chest. Suzie decided he must be feeling better. She hoped he was feeling better.

Arlene Miller, the head nurse in the ICU, saw Dr. Hauser bring Suzie into Jimmy's cubicle and watched as she left. Nurse Miller thought Jimmy's girl looked calmer than she would have expected, as though she did not realize he was going to die.

By escorting Suzie into the ICU, Dr. Hauser unintentionally broke the monopoly Jimmy's mother held on visiting privileges. At 2:00 P.M., time for another visit, Suzie went in again. She thought Jimmy looked better. He began to write her notes on the plastic pad. He normally had illegible handwriting, and in his weakened condition his writing became almost impossible to read. Suzie noticed Jimmy become irritated when she failed to read his notes.

One of them said "hot." She felt his forehead, and he was indeed hot.

"Where's Dr. Hauser?" Suzie asked the nurse.

"He'll be back soon," said the nurse. "The doctor thought Jimmy looked better, so he left to attend to other business."

"I think his temperature's up."

"I'll check it, but you're going to have to leave."

Suzie looked in Jimmy's eyes. He looked frightened. He did not want her to leave, but she told him she had to. She went out to the waiting room.

Jimmy's mother visited him the next hour. Even while donning her gown, mask, and gloves before entering the cubicle, she could see Jimmy motioning for her to hurry. He wanted to tell her something, but she could not understand. Finally, the nurse handed him the plastic pad and he wrote, "Get Dr. Hauser." Then he motioned for his mother to go quickly. She went out into the waiting room and told Uncle Red to call Dr. Hauser.

Dr. Hauser had already been called. At 3:00 Nurse Miller noticed on the electrocardiogram scope that Jimmy's heart tracings changed into a left bundle block pattern. The left chamber of the heart had begun to fail. His condition immediately started to deteriorate. Dr. Hauser arrived at the unit almost immediately, accompanied by a cardiologist. Jimmy still could not talk because of the tracheotomy tube in his neck, but he could mouth words. Dr. Hauser asked him, "Is there anything I can do for you?"

"There's nothing you can do for me," mouthed Jimmy Caruthers. "Just get me out of here!"

But the pneumonia raging within him had begun to overcome the resistance provided by the antibiotics, and his lungs steadily filled with mucus. Dr. Hauser adjusted the switch on the oxygen machine, turning it higher, forcing increasingly higher percentages of oxygen into Jimmy's stuffed lungs, hoping to saturate the lungs with pure oxygen so that it would reach the bloodstream despite the mucus blocking its route. Finally the oxygen could not be turned any higher.

At 4:15 P.M. Jimmy Caruthers' heart stopped. The cardiologist quickly gave him an injection of heart-stimulating drugs. He also shocked the heart with electric paddles and succeeded in obtaining a response. The heart began to beat again.

Jimmy opened his eyes, a dead man returned momentarily from the grave and looked at Dr. Hauser. "You're doing fine," Dr. Hauser told him. "Everything is going fine."

Jimmy smiled.

But his heart stopped again. Once more the doctors labored to restimulate the heart, to get it beating once again. They failed. At 4:45 P.M. on October 26, 1975, the electrocardiographic monitor connected to room thirteen in the intensive care unit of Tustin Community Hospital showed only a straight line.

When Dr. Hauser walked into the waiting area and told Suzie Grim that Jimmy Caruthers was dead, she at first did not believe him. "You're kidding," she said. She knew Jimmy was extremely sick, but somehow the idea never entered her mind that he would die. Jimmy's mother and father went into the intensive care unit to see their dead son, but Suzie decided to remain outside.

Later, after Jimmy's mother returned, Suzie Grim put her arm around Mrs. Caruthers' shoulder and tried to console her. "I loved your son," she said.

Jimmy's mother stared straight ahead: "I loved him, too."

Kay Smith, the head nurse from the pediatrics floor, learned of Jimmy's death when she walked into the cafeteria. Several nurses were so upset that they were crying. She joined them. Her husband came by later that evening with her four-year-old boy to take her home. She told her husband about the death of her patient and began to cry again.

"Who died, Mom?" her four-year-old boy (whose name happened to be Jim) wanted to know.

"Jimmy died."

"I didn't die, Mom."

"Never mind, Sweetheart."

Her husband asked, "Why are you so upset over a patient?"

"I can't help it," she replied.

"I didn't die, Mom," her young son repeated.

Jerry McClung and Jim Williams went fishing in the mountains north of Phoenix that weekend and returned home late Sunday night. Their camper contained a television set in the back tuned to the evening news. They were not watching the set, but the sound remained on. The announcer said, "This afternoon Indianapolis race driver Jimmy Caruthers lost his final race. He died of cancer."

McClung pulled the camper over to the side of the road.

"I didn't even know he was back in the hospital," said Williams.

Lee Kunzman raced in Birmingham, Alabama, that afternoon and afterwards called the hospital to talk to his friend. "I'm sorry, but we can't give you any information on Mr. Caruthers," said the hospital operator. "His family isn't here."

"I don't want to talk to his family," said Lee, irritated. "I just want to talk to Jim."

"I'm sorry, but his family isn't here."

Kunzman finally telephoned Doug and learned.

Later that evening Gene Romero returned with Nancy from their trip. It had been a short, but good, vacation.

Burritto had visited his parents, had stopped by to see a motorcycle racer injured in a fall, then spent the weekend in Reno. While unloading the van he heard the telephone ring inside the apartment. Nancy answered it. "Doug wants to talk to you," she said. Doug told Burritto the news.

The next morning Shirley Fitzpatrick came to work. She examined the hospital census to see which room Jimmy was in because she thought she might stop by and say hello. She could not find Jimmy's name and at first thought that puzzling, then remembered Jimmy's chemotherapy was due to end that weekend. She turned to Dick Bell, the chief technician in the X-ray department and said, "Jimmy must have gone home."

Bell shook his head: "He didn't go home."

The wake for Jimmy Caruthers lasted two days. Doug visited the funeral parlor the first day. Jimmy's mother and the other members of the family did not attend the wake. Suzie Grim spent both days at the funeral parlor by herself.

She ordered the arrangements for the funeral. The flowers, in best racing tradition, were black and white. Jimmy's helmet had been placed atop a pedestal. The coffin was metallic gray with silver trimming, sharp-looking, streamlined, as though capable of two hundred miles per hour down the straightaway, lacking only racing decals. Jimmy Caruthers lay inside, dressed in his racing uniform.

Jimmy's racing friends came to the funeral: Lee Kunzman, Johnny Rutherford. Bob Fletcher appeared and frowned when he saw his driver, Billy Vukovich, dressed in Levis.

Lee Kunzman sat through the services, staring at Jimmy's coffin. He stared and he waited. He had a weird idea he could not get out of his mind. He half expected that any minute Jimmy Caruthers, dressed in his driver's uniform

251

would sit up in that coffin and start laughing: "Hahahaha-ha. I fooled you! It's a joke. I'm not really dead!" Lee Kunzman knew Jimmy might pull a trick like that and walk out the door of the funeral home laughing his head off.

But, of course, he never did.

Epilogue

Suzie Grim continued her job as a TWA stewardess, flying out of O'Hare Field in Chicago. She moved to a new apartment in Schaumburg, a small suburb of Chicago not far from the airport. "I loved Jimmy dearly," she said. "I always will. We only had five years together, but it was enough to fill a lifetime." Recently she married another race driver.

Doug Caruthers moved away from California. The summer after his son's death he and Dana bought a house in Indianapolis, west of the Speedway, on a large plot of ground overlooking the expressway. At the USAC banquet in January 1976 he accepted the award for his son's dirt car championship won the previous summer. It was only the second time in USAC history that a championship was awarded posthumously to a driver. The first time, of course, involved Danny Caruthers. "This is very beautiful," said Doug, accepting the plaque, "and I know that Jimmy would be real happy to receive this. There are a lot of things I would like to say tonight, but I just don't feel like saying a lot." When he stepped down there were tears in the eyes of many people.

Soon after Jimmy's death, his mother stopped by the hospital to pick up his belongings, including the attaché case with the picture of his championship car on one side, his midget racer on the other. As she was leaving, Nurse Mary Hill indicated a plant sent to Jimmy during his last sickness. The plant included a spider plant and defavaccia with a tiny American flag stuck in the dirt. "What do you want to do with this plant?" Mary Hill asked Jimmy's mother.

"I don't know," Mrs. Caruthers replied.

So the nurses kept it, and placed it on the counter in front of their station in the pediatrics ward and watered it daily. The plant continues to grow.